# Praise for
# "Teach Skills and Break Habits"

The shift in perspective Dan provides is huge. There are subtle changes in the way you can address students that have huge impact on their behavior. Instead of assuming students 'know better' and punishing them for not having the appropriate social behaviors, Dan equips us to teach them these skills and practice them.

**Tara Mesing, Virginia Beach, VA**

Dan's approach has been a game changer for me. As a ⌐ teacher I was struggling to find a behavior manager that would meet multiple needs in my classroom gave me the tools I needed to create a be⊬ for my students. I use the callbacks with are a great way to remind them of regulating their own behavior.

I cannot thank Dan enough for the pe⌐ ⌐s brought me. Yes, I will always have 'those' kids. ⊾ ⌐n better prepared and equipped to help them m⊾ ⌐r potential.

**Sara Umphries, West Terre Haute, IN**

After hearing Dan speak three years ago about behavior management, everything suddenly made sense to me. We teach everything else to children in stages, why not behavior? I immediately went back to my room and threw out my "card system." I explained the system being gone to my class and one of my students said, "I am so happy nobody will have to change their ticket anymore. That made me so sad."

I continue to apply Dan's approach to teach classes and parent's each year. His model creates accountability to the entire class; they use the callbacks on each other. My personal favorite is when they get in each other's space and say, "I have my space, you have your space." It creates mutual respect in my room. I wish I had known Dan 25 years ago when I first started teaching!

**Susan Evans, Atlantic Highlands, NJ**

*My second year teaching was rough. I started the year on maternity leave and had several challenging behaviors: hitting, screaming, crying, throwing, and constant blurting. I sincerely questioned whether to return to teaching the next year.*

*My first ah-ha! moment was when Dan likened behaviors to academics. If a child cannot read, we teach. If our teaching is unsuccessful, we scaffold and make accommodations until the child grows. Why were we punishing behavior instead of teaching it?*

*When I changed my approach, I found that I no longer felt like I needed to yell, and I was able to see the change in behavior I was looking for more quickly. My stress level decreased by a landslide.*

**Crystal Weaver, Apple Valley, CA**


*Dan taught me that behavior change happens in relationship.*

*When thinking of interventions, I regularly remind myself that my goal is behavior change. I constantly ask if the intervention I intend to use can be expected to achieve the behavior change I am seeking.*

**Rachel Gurwitz, San Antonio, TX**


*After many years of teaching, and struggling with challenging behaviors, Dan's teachings completely changed my thinking and my classroom for the better.I said goodbye to my clip chart and began teaching Dan's lessons, and practicing the skills. His ways are so logical, and simple to implement. Practice time occurs regularly in my classroom, and it works.*

**Amy Wallace, Robbinsville, NJ**


*I attended one of Dan's workshops and everything made so much sense. My classroom environment is much different now than before. It is more fun and enjoyable as I look at behavior as a skill to be mastered instead of trying to control behavior through moving a pin on a chart. We have moved away from trying to be good to "earn a sticker or color," to trying to be good because it is the right thing to do.*

**Kari McHone, Boerne, TX**


*Dan's presentations and books have helped me see student behavior in a new way, and to understand that teaching behavioral skills, step by step, helps a child in all areas.*

**Laurie Drummond, Nashville, TN**

# Duplication and Copyright

NCYI titles may be purchased in bulk at special discounts for educational, business, fundraising, or promotional use. For more information, please email sales@ncyi.org.

NATIONAL CENTER for
**YOUTH ISSUES**

P.O. Box 22185 • Chattanooga, TN 37422-2185
423-899-5714 • 866-318-6294 • fax: 423-899-4547
www.ncyi.org

ISBN: 978-1937870492   $19.95
Library of Congress Control Number: 2018944190
© 2018 National Center for Youth Issues, Chattanooga, TN
All rights reserved.

Written by: Dan St. Romain
Contributing Editor: Jennifer Deshler • Design: Phillip Rodgers
Published by National Center for Youth Issues

Printed at LSC Communications, Harrisonburg, Virginia, U.S.A.
June 2018

# Teach Skills

## ——— AND ———

# Break Habits

## Growth Mindsets
## for Better Behavior
## in the Classroom

Published by

NATIONAL CENTER for
YOUTH ISSUES

# Dedication

I am forever grateful to the staff at the Howard Early Childhood Center in the Alamo Heights Independent School District in San Antonio, Texas. Over the course of the last fifteen years in working with them, they have shown me that not only is there a better way to deal with discipline in the school system, but that it can be done. Their flexibility in meeting the behavioral needs our students, willingness to challenge assumptions, and continual openness to growth encouraged me to write this book.

# Contents

# Letter to Reader

This body of work has been in my brain for almost a decade, waiting to get out. Each time I tried to organize my thoughts and begin typing, I discovered gaps in my understanding. Until now. Somehow, this past year, the stars aligned and I began to see how all the pieces of the puzzle fit together.

The bottom line: Behavior is complicated. And when we try to simplify it, we often miss the mark. I believe this is the frustration of many teachers who have been given simple strategies for complex behaviors. If you are picking up this book, you are probably one of these teachers. And I'm guessing you are looking for more effective strategies.

Over the last several months, I've had the opportunity to work with an amazing group of educators from Virginia Public Schools on the issue of student behavior and social emotional learning. After providing several staff development sessions, in-class modeling, and consultation, I met with the staff to examine the outcome of our efforts.

After a few meetings, I realized I was getting the same feedback from each group. The teachers were most thankful for the opportunity to examine student behaviors in a new way, and for being given specific strategies to teach behavioral skills and break poor habits. They had shifted their own perspectives, and were more receptive to trying different strategies to change behaviors.

Not surprisingly, that is the focus of this book: Changing perspectives to change behaviors. As you read the book and see this icon, I encourage you to remember the importance of examining your beliefs about student behavior - as I believe this is the first step, and ultimately the best means, of creating positive behavioral change in your students.

**Dan St. Romain**

# CHAPTER ONE

# Changing With the Times

> *Oh, the things you can find if you don't stay behind!* – DR. SEUSS

**Our son, Micah,** was six years old when he entered kindergarten. We had strategically waited an extra year to give him time to mature socially and emotionally before he enrolled. At his former day care, they told us as long as Micah's new teacher kept him busy, he would be fine. Yes, Micah was a "busy bee." My wife and I suspected that his *proclivity for activity* would no doubt be an issue of concern in the classroom. Since my wife taught at the same school, she warned the kindergarten teacher about his behavior. (Did I mention this was her first year teaching at the school?) She was young, smart, energetic, and had a dynamic presence, so we thought: *"if anyone can keep up with Micah in kindergarten, it will be her."*

During the first week of school, Micah brought home a behavior folder that provided us with daily feedback. Initially, Micah received "plus" marks, indicating he had good days. We were optimistic, but our optimism was short lived. By the end of the first week, "minuses," indicating behavior concerns, started to pop up. Of course, my wife and I sat Micah down and tried to encourage positive behavior, but the efforts yielded little success. Although he had some good days, the minuses he received clearly out-weighed the pluses. Micah also began conveniently leaving his folder on the bus at the end of each day. He would explain, *"Daddy, I don't know where my folder is. It must be in the classroom, but I had a good day!"* His teacher heard a variation of this same theme: *"My folder? It must be in my mom's car."*

Although my wife and I continued to work with Micah on making good choices, his problems in the classroom persisted. On the third week of school, after several "minus" days, my wife called to let me know Micah had snuck back into his classroom at the end of the day and emptied the contents of his teacher's prize box of stickers and pencils into his backpack. Yes. Our child was now a thief.

That evening, when we spoke with Micah, he asked, *"Why am I always the one in trouble?"* He told us some kids wouldn't play with him anymore at school because he was the *"bad kid."* After some probing, we discovered he was giving out the stolen pencils and stickers from the prize box to kids in his class - so they would play with him. It seemed our son was working the system to buy back his friends.

As a parent, I didn't know what to say. I was exceedingly frustrated with his behavior, but I also knew (to a certain extent), he was *trying* to do the right thing and was just unable to live up to the established expectations. We knew Micah had behavior issues. We knew he had the right teacher. We knew she really liked Micah and was doing everything she could to help him succeed. But, somehow, things were definitely going awry.

At this point, we were very worried about Micah's self-esteem, which was dropping. We were also worried about his relationships with peers, which were clearly damaged. We took him to the doctor, as we felt confident we knew the source of the problem. Micah was diagnosed with Attention Deficit Hyperactivity Disorder (ADHD) and started medication that fall. We were very fortunate his behavior improved dramatically. Don't get me wrong, he still had social skill deficits and other behavioral concerns that needed to be addressed, but too a much more manageable degree. Although I was pleased there was an improvement in his behavior, I remember thinking, *"What if the medication didn't work? Would Micah still be getting minuses every day?"*

In three short weeks, my son went from loving school and having friends, to feeling singled out, isolated, and always in trouble. I could not see how this was possible. As an educator, I also intuitively understood that Micah couldn't be the only child facing this challenge. I was left wondering, *"How many other children and parents are having this same experience?"*

## So, What's the Problem?

Over the past twenty years, I have heard many variations of Micah's situation from countless parents and teachers. I've listened to story after story of students struggling with behavioral and emotional concerns, and their teachers finding little success with interventions. Unfortunately, the theme of behavior problems in the school system is all too common. I hear the same sentiment repeatedly from teachers across the country:

*"If I could just teach, I'd be fine. But my school day feels like a continuous game of 'whack-a-mole' with small amounts of teaching squeezed in. I spend all my time dealing with behavior issues and it drives me nuts!"*

It seems more and more teachers are living in survival mode, trying their best to deal with classroom behaviors, while meeting the academic needs of their students. The problem is only exacerbated by the nation's continual hyper-focus on testing and increased rigor in the school system. Don't get me wrong, I'm all for having high academic standards, but there needs to be a balance. We need to make certain our practices are developmentally appropriate, and it is critical we take into consideration other aspects of children's well-being, (in addition to cognition); specifically, their social and emotional needs.

When I ask parents about the goals they have for their children, the responses are usually the same: "*I want my child to like school…be happy and well-adjusted…be a life-long learner, and make friends.*" Over the course of several decades, I have yet to hear a parent tell me: "*I want my child to have high test scores.*" I find it ironic that having exemplary test scores is the primary goal found on most Campus Improvement Plans. Yes, for most schools, the primary focus seems to be on meeting the academic benchmarks we set, often at the expense of everything else. The obvious problem with this line of thinking is that if we don't support the social and emotional needs of our students, the cognitive goals achieved will mean very little when they are older. Children who can't behave grow into adults who can't behave.

Educators don't disagree, but seem to be at a loss for how best to deal with behavior problems in the classroom:

> Dan says…
>
> *Children who can't behave grow into adults who can't behave.*

> *I tried everything. I spent all my time signing folders, giving out stickers, and moving clips, but I still had tons of behavior problems. Nothing seemed to work.*
>
> – L. Vincent

*Nothing worked...*and therein lies the problem – continual interventions with minimal success.

## The Times – They are a-Changin'

Unfortunately, when it comes to working with the current behavior problems we are facing in schools, our interventions don't seem to be working as well as they once did. In part, this is due to changes that have taken place in our society over the last few decades. And these changes have had a huge impact on children's behaviors. The best way to understand the impact is to examine the changes themselves.

### Behavioral Expectations

To this day, I still remember a vacation I took with my family when I was a teen. Truth be known, it wasn't so much the vacation I recall, but rather the flight to and from our destination. When I learned we were going to Jamaica, I filled my luggage with all the necessities: tank tops, bathing suits, and flip-flops. It was only after I packed that my mother asked me if I had my *jacket and tie* laid out for the flight. Huh? Yes,

I had to wear a suit on the plane. Everybody did so, as that was the standard. We also had to dress up for church and nice dinners. Wearing nice attire was the expected behavior in many settings.

Needless to say, those standards have changed dramatically. We are less formal and less defined with regard to our behavior expectations. And it's not just the way we dress; as a society, we have adopted a more casual approach to everything. Our word choice is more casual. Our attitude is more casual. And as is very apparent, student behaviors in the classroom are more casual.

## Role Models

When we are young, we learn about behaviors by watching and interacting with others. The individuals around us have a huge impact on our behavior, as they serve as role models. My primary role models were my parents. In addition to mom and dad, I looked up to other individuals on television to teach me about life. Pop culture icons like Gomer Pyle, Beaver Cleaver, Bobby Brady, and Batman shaped my behavior. By watching them on TV, I learned unspoken rules about societal expectations, how to interact with others, and yes, how to behave. Their behaviors influenced my idea of "normal."

We don't have to look far to realize current role models have redefined behavioral norms. Today's pop culture icons behave very differently than they did in past decades. Pick three popular television shows and watch them. If you make a list of some of the behaviors modeled, the point will be evident. Language, sarcasm, violence - adult themes in mass media - have increased, and the changes have had a dramatic influence on the behavior of children.

## Interaction with Others

When I was younger, I spent the majority of my time after school outside with friends. We hung out on the playground, rode our bikes, played basketball, ran around the neighborhood, or played "Kick the Can" and "Red Light Green Light." These games and activities taught me very important life lessons:

- ➤ I don't always get what I want.
- ➤ People sometimes say mean things.
- ➤ Life isn't always fair.
- ➤ Sometimes I win. Sometimes I lose.

By playing with others, I also learned how to disagree, work through conflict, compromise, play nicely, and share. These were critical life skills and I learned them through daily interactions with my peers.

In today's society, kids have a great deal of screen time, and when they are in front of screens, they are not practicing face-to-face communication. Technology is a great tool, but it can never

**Dan says...**

*Technology is a great tool, but it can never replace human interaction...*

replace human interaction, which naturally provides opportunities to learn social skills. This deficit is often evidenced through children's behaviors.

## Messages

The unspoken messages I learned from adults when I was young were quite clear:

- Leave things nicer than you found them.
- Mind your manners.
- Say "please" and "thank you."
- Respect your elders.

There was no confusion about *how* I was expected to act, as adults sent consistent messages regarding our beliefs and behaviors. The values I learned had the same themes of respect and compliance. I was taught "The Golden Rule": treat others the way you want to be treated. I was also taught to do what I was told. Whether these were good messages or not, they were at least consistent. My friends and I knew how to behave since the adults seemed to have a unified voice in their expectations.

Consistent messages were also easier to come by, due to our dependence on each other. The neighbors knew my family (and they watched out for me), so I couldn't do anything without word getting back to my mother and father. Families relied on each other to collectively raise kids. The more everyone communicated, the easier it was to send consistent messages about behavioral expectations.

However, we have moved from a society of dependence to independence, with more working families and individuals raising children in isolation than ever before. Neighbors don't know each other as well and we have more single parents raising children. These changes have had an impact on the messages we send to our kids, with one parent teaching, "think before you speak," and another teaching, "just do it." Yes - these mixed messages have negatively influenced kid's behaviors.

**Hold that Thought...**

I'm not trying to imply that change is bad. The progress we have made over the last half-century is staggering. Advances in technology, equal rights, acceptance of differences, and health care have all had a positive effect on our society. Nevertheless, we must acknowledge how these changes have impacted student's attention levels, social interactions, and emotional health. This does not mean we excuse inappropriate behavior. Nor does it mean we should to go back to the "Good Ole' Days" before technology. However, if we don't understand where the behavior comes from, we can't effectively find the best solutions.

# Three Strikes – You're Out

Our inclination is to discipline kids the way we were once disciplined - as both a teacher and dad that is exactly what I did. I adopted many of the same methods of punishment my own parents and teachers used, which I later learned was not always the best approach.

When I first started teaching, I worked in a residential treatment facility for children and teens with severe behavior concerns. My first thought was to use an assertive discipline, "take control" kind of approach. As you might imagine, this did not work out, given the population with which I worked. Every day, I ended up in power struggles with my students. It seemed the more I asserted my authority, the more behaviors escalated: **Strike One!**

I also worked for a brief period in the "adjustment" room. The name alone should have given me pause. This was a place students could be sent, in lieu of the office, when behaviors reached an unmanageable point in the classroom. Although the idea of this time-out approach was to help students adjust their attitude and reflect on their choices, the room operated more as a detention or holding cell. Students stayed in cubbies either sleeping or doing schoolwork until they were ready to go back to class. Of course, in a room staffed with counselors trained to work with this population, the outcome might be different. This, however, was not the case. When students were out of control or not compliant, they were often restrained. The room was explained to me as a therapeutic place, but the practices seemed to align more with a philosophy of behavior control rather than reflection and self-regulation. Looking back on my lack of skills, and the somewhat tragic results of my work in that room, I cringe. **Strike Two!**

When I left that job and relocated to Texas, I interviewed for a teaching position in a small public school district. The school had an opening in their Academic Compliance Training (ACT) program for youth with behavior problems. As I understood it, whenever students misbehaved they would be taken to my room, where I would give them an ACT packet of schoolwork to complete as punishment. If students misbehaved while in the room, I was to add another page to their already lengthy packet. This was to be the case for every infraction. The job requirements were that I not speak with the students, but just continue to pass out pages if they misbehaved. Students were to stay with me until all the pages in their packet were completed and therefore "compliance" was achieved. *"Do you have any questions?"* I was asked after the interview. I was completely speechless and disturbed... on so many levels.

I walked out of that interview scratching my head. All I could think about was horse training. From what I could gather, the job was to "break" the students in an effort to train them. This was a philosophy I simply could not adopt. Though I'm sure the strategy was well-intended, I knew I could not in good conscience carry out that job. **Strike Three!**

"*Surely, compliance can't be the answer,*" I thought. And that was the very moment in my career when I became professionally committed to finding a better way. Little did I realize the stakes would get much higher for me years later, once I became a dad.

## There is a Better Way

My brother-in-law once told me, "*Your firstborn is a gift from God to show you all the love in the world. Your second born is a gift from God to show you there is still evil to be overcome.*" Although he said this in jest, I do believe my second child was a gift from God to teach me how to be a better dad. You see, although I didn't get much experience in dealing with oppositional behaviors with my oldest child, Micah more than pulled his weight in helping me understand the ineffectiveness of my behavior strategies. Traditional methods that seemed to work with my oldest had little effect on Micah. I could send him to his room or put him in time-out for extended periods, but neither intervention seemed to change his behavior. Every time Micah went to time-out, I felt the pain of the intervention not working. Slowly, I began to understand behavior in a different way – in my work as educator, in my experience as a dad, and most importantly, through the eyes of my own struggling son. I had to learn the hard way I could not change my child's behavior, or the behavior of the students I taught without first changing my own.

Fast-forward twenty years, and I'm writing this book, which is based on a very specific and pressing need. We must find a better way to support children's behaviors in the school setting. After years of practice, I have learned there truly *is* a better way. However, I must throw out a warning before you turn another page: While this book contains ideas for creating positive behavior change in the classroom, the biggest change I hope to make is one of mindset... *your* mindset. My own "aha" moment came in realizing that strategies alone could not solve my problems. As a dad and teacher, I had to adjust my own perspective. Though it presented huge obstacles for me, over the years I've grown exponentially in my understanding and practices toward dealing with challenging behaviors. If you are ready to question your belief system and current practices, I encourage you to read on, as I believe this information can radically impact the way you approach behavior in your classroom.

CHAPTER TWO

# Avoiding System Failure

**George was a fourth grader** with a history of behavioral problems. He had impulsivity issues, and could easily fly off the handle and let out a string of expletives, should things not go his way. He regularly visited the office, usually because he needed a place to cool down. This office time helped both George and his teacher regroup. Unfortunately, the behavior system the fourth grade teachers used did not work for him. Each day, students received marks in their agendas indicating how well they behaved. As part of their homework, the students were expected to have these agendas signed by their parents. Upon returning the signed agendas to their teachers each day, students received "behavior bucks" that could be used to purchase items from the "class store." George's frequent failure to bring back the agenda led to him receiving very few bucks, which meant he rarely had enough money to buy anything from the store. This frustrated both George and his teachers:

*"If he would just get the agenda signed, he could get the bucks. He's never going to survive when he is in the fifth grade if he can't even remember to get his daily agenda signed this year."*

George was in a very bad behavior cycle. His extreme actions earned him negative marks, daily. When his parents saw the marks in the folder, George got in trouble, so he avoided showing it to them. Of course, when George returned to school without the agenda, he did not earn behavior bucks, which led to more frustration and more problems. George wanted behavior bucks, but his agenda was a constant reminder of his bad behavior. The other students' successes only made him angrier. I felt bad for George. He *wanted* to be successful. Not only did he tell me this on several occasions, but he also beamed about his success on the rare days he received good marks in that folder. Although I empathized with his teacher who struggled with his behaviors, I knew one thing for sure: the system was not working for George.

# Do You Need to Move Your Clip?

Classroom management systems come in all shapes and sizes. A popular one that gained traction over the last few decades is *The Clip Chart*. I learned about it when I first began working at an early childhood center. With this system, each classroom has a clip chart, and when students follow the classroom expectations, their clips [clothespins] are placed in the green section of the chart. If a child misbehaves, he or she receives a warning and the clip is moved to the yellow section of the chart. If problems persist, the clip is moved to the red section, at which point the child receives a time-out or some other negative consequence. Periodically, when all clips remain in the green section of the chart, the class receives rewards and incentives, such as stickers, "warm fuzzies" (small tokens), or a class celebration.

I had a gut-level negative response to the charts, probably because of my experience as a parent of a "red" clip kid. I really respected these teachers, and knew they were very good at their jobs. They understood developmentally appropriate practices, were child-centered, great at building relationships, and worked for high achievement. Still, something didn't sit well with me about this behavior system.

From the outset, two of the teachers let me know they didn't like the charts, but did not know what to do instead. I remember one of them saying,

*"It breaks my heart that Michael doesn't want to come to school because he's going to have to move his clip."* Other teachers told me they liked the system, but were frustrated because the same kids repeatedly had to move their clips for misbehavior - an observation that was hard to miss since the charts were prominently displayed in the classrooms.

Although I was charged with supporting behavior efforts at the school, I did my best to refrain from offering opinions unless they were solicited. I took a back door approach and supported individual teachers who approached me. Slowly, over the course of about ten years, the culture of the behavioral climate changed, and one by one, the clip systems and other punishment/reward strategies were abandoned. The principal did not mandate their removal at any point. Teachers became open to handling discipline in a different way, mostly because they came to the same conclusion: Student behaviors seemed to be getting worse, yet the systems being used were not working, nor did they align with our school's ever-evolving beliefs. Something had to change.

## This Too Shall Pass

Change is a common theme in schools. Educators who have worked in the field for a while know if you are going to survive in the school system, you have to be able to deal with change - especially when it comes to the adoption of new initiatives. As a teacher once told me, *"Our school jumps from program to program, looking for just the right one, but the results are always the same. Just when we start to get comfortable with one, the pendulum swings, a new initiative comes along, and we are on a new adventure. When we start a new program, I often think to myself, 'Just wait. This too shall pass.'"* Sound familiar?

Although change can be frustrating, it is necessary. I believe this is why administrators adopt new systems and programs - to keep up with the trends and patterns of our ever-changing society. As the world around us changes, so must we grow and adapt. This is why we need to examine the strategies being used to change behaviors. Student behaviors surely have transformed - have our strategies kept up? In the first chapter, we looked at changes in our society impacting the behavior of our kids. One change we have yet to examine is that of our own interventions.

## Please, Don't Call My Momma!

In classrooms of days gone by, teachers used mostly compliance-based methods of classroom management to reduce poor behavior with phrases like, *"Stop talking. Stop moving. Stop misbehaving."* These types of comments and accompanying strategies were based on the *"because I said* so" mindset. Many *mature* adults can remember classmates having to lean down and touch their toes while being introduced to the paddle. Or writing lines such as, *"I will not talk. I will not talk."* Staying after school to do manual labor was quite common, as well. Of course, *I* never had to do it, but some of my classmates did have to scrape gum off the bottom of desks, clean scuff marks off the floors, and pick up trash on the playground. These types of punishment-based responses to poor behavior were the norm.

Now, before we go on, I believe it is important to note that for the most part, these strategies were effective in stopping misbehavior. Make no mistake, when I was in school, I did *not* want to be sent out in the hall. I did *not* want to stand in the corner. And for Heaven's sake, *please* don't call my momma! These interventions were used sparingly when needed, and generally yielded the desired outcome: the inappropriate behaviors stopped.

## The Same Strategies with Different Packaging

In today's classroom, we still have consequences for misbehavior - they just look different and are a bit more sophisticated and time-consuming. Now we have a whole host of packaged programs and systems on the market to help teachers deal with behaviors in the classroom. Popular ones include:

- Behavior Folders
- Red-Light/Green Light Systems
- Class Dojo
- Color/Clip Charts
- Behavior Bucks
- Time-Out
- Marble Jars

These systems and strategies focus on *negative* reinforcement (punishment) by attempting to discourage misbehavior, and/or positive reinforcement (rewards) to encourage desired behaviors. Those based in punishment are of the same mindset we have used for decades. The underlying message: *"If you don't like the consequences, then you need to behave."*

## How's that Working for You?

As we have established the reasoning behind these strategies, our next step is look at the results of our efforts. When examining the effectiveness of behavior systems or strategies, I find classroom kiddos usually fall into three categories:

### The "Good" Ones

Students in this category tend to be well-behaved. While they occasionally have to be redirected, they generally follow expectations and make good choices. These tend to be the students for whom the strategies and behavior systems work. They always have positive marks in their behavior folder, receive stickers, and earn behavior bucks. These students have the unspoken label as The "Good" Kids. (Did you feel me cringe as I typed those last three words?)

### The "Followers"

Students in this category tend to need a higher degree of support. Although the behaviors they exhibit might not be considered severe, they can present a challenge to the classroom teacher, who must spend more time throughout the day redirecting them. I tend to believe these kiddos follow the excitement. If students around them are making good choices and doing well, they often follow suit. However, if poor choices are being made, they can just as easily jump on the "crazy train," and misbehave. These students' behaviors are manageable; however, the strategies or systems applied in the classroom can be the determining factor in their success or failure.

### The "Bad" Ones

These students exhibit behaviors that could be categorized as severe (as evidenced by the behavior's frequency, duration, and intensity). The needs of these students take up a great deal of the teacher's energy and effort, often at the expense of the other students in the class. Students in this category are those for whom the system or strategies don't seem to work. They regularly receive the associated negative consequences while rarely, if ever, earning rewards. These students have the understood, unspoken label of *The "Bad" Kids*. (Again, cringing as I type this.)

When examining these three groups of students, a disturbing pattern becomes evident. It seems our

> Dan says...
>
> *It seems our systems are not changing the behaviors of the very students for whom they were designed.*

systems are not changing the behaviors of the very students for whom they were designed. Walk into any classroom and you will note the same students receiving *all* of the redirection...with minimal system success. Often referred to as the behavioral "frequent flyers," these students are continually sent to the office or time-out, due to the ineffectiveness of our classroom interventions.

> *It was always the same students that received the same consequences – and when that happened over and over again, those kids felt defeated and just gave up. It made me sad because I never want any of my students feeling singled out or disconnected from our class, because they are always in trouble.*
>
> – M. Johnson

Many teachers can point out the high percentage of students (the *"Good"* Ones) for whom punishment and reward systems are working. Though many *do* find success, it is important to remember the systems were not designed with these students in mind. If we were to take away the systems, these students would still be well behaved. These students tend to have an internal locus of control motivating them to do the right thing, simply because it is the right thing to do. They have developed healthy behavioral habits and act accordingly.

## To *Change* or *Contain*: That is the Question

When examining interventions in education, I often use the prison system as a sad comparison to the discipline efforts in our schools. If our desired outcome is to *contain* behavior, we are doing okay, but we had better build prisons faster, as we are not keeping up with the demand. Our prison population is overflowing. If our only goal is to remove and isolate an individual from society, we can continue our current practices, but we will also need to put more money and effort in to creating more prisons and hiring more employees to staff them. If our goal is to *change* the behaviors of the incarcerated, we are doing an abysmal job, as evidenced by the high recidivism rates. Within five years of being released, roughly three-quarters of prisoners return to jail, and more than half return within in the first year. Clearly, prisons are not meeting the goal of reforming behavior.

The same seems to hold true for our behavioral interventions in the school system. We might be containing behavior, but change is not as evident. The *same* students seem to be receiving the *same* interventions continuously. If the main goal of an intervention is to change behavior, we have to acknowledge that many of our current strategies and systems, especially those relying on punishment and rewards, are simply *not* working. In fact, many times, the opposite is true. In an attempt to change behavior, we sometimes damage relationships because we lose sight of *how* students receive our interventions. Perhaps if we put ourselves in the shoes of our students, we will be in a better position to see things from their perspective.

## What if We Started "Clipping" Teachers?

How would you respond if, as a teacher, you went to your box in the workroom and discovered your administrator had adopted the clip system? All staff members had been rated with one of the three clips: green, yellow, or red. If you received a green clip, I imagine you might secretly do the happy dance, but not tell a soul, as you wouldn't want to be labeled "the principal's favorite" by the rest of the staff. If you had a yellow clip, you might be mad or embarrassed, nervously laugh with the rest of the staff, and do what you needed to get to green. If, however, you were tagged with the red clip, things could get ugly fast. Perhaps you would go straight to the store and purchase a whole bag of red clips to "decorate" the box, showing your principal the full extent of your *red clip* potential. I would think most teachers would be livid that they were not only rated, but publically humiliated, as well.

To some degree, this happened to my wife early in her teaching career. Her principal expected teachers to be in their classrooms at 7:00 a.m., which proved to be a challenge for my wife and a few of her colleagues. In an attempt to change faculty behaviors, at 7:01 a.m. each morning, the principal highlighted the names of the teachers on the sign-in sheet who had arrived late. My wife's first passive-aggressive response was to take the initiative and highlight her own name on the following day's sign-in sheet before leaving each evening – which I'm certain, was not the response the principal was hoping for. My wife didn't have a problem with being expected to be at work on time, but the intervention the principal used was damaging their relationship. I believe this same type of scenario often plays out in classrooms as students demonstrate compliant behaviors, but at the cost of healthy teacher-student relationships.

# The Behavioral Golden Rule

There is a better way. And it begins with this premise: Discipline students the way you would want to be disciplined. I use this same "Behavioral

> Dan says...
>
> *Discipline students the way you would want to be disciplined.*

Golden Rule" when I am the "teacher" providing staff development to adults. Just as I would never want to be singled out for talking during professional development (or for coming in late), I wouldn't think of doing so to participants in my sessions. My goal is to think about how I would want to be treated, and treat my students the same way – which is my challenge to you. I believe that given most of the current strategies and behavior systems used today, this is a *radically* different approach. If we choose to keep using the same strategies we have been using, very little will change. Continuing on the same course is the definition of insanity – doing the same thing over and over again and expecting different results.

I invite you to consider an approach that starts with assessing our desired outcomes. I believe we should *begin with the end in mind* and look at the specific outcomes we are trying to achieve with our interventions. By doing so, we can make sure we are all headed in the same direction, and have a great way to measure the effectiveness of the support we hope to provide along the way.

CHAPTER TWO

 CHAPTER THREE

# ASSESSING OUTCOMES

## The Problem With TTWWADI's

Tootie Byrd was a wonderful eighty year-old humorist who often spoke at educational conferences and shared her insights about life and education. She famously talked about people's TTWWADI's getting in the way of change. *That's The Way We've Always Done It.* As she often said, *"We do what we know, and we do what we've done – even when it's not working."* When it comes to our behavior interventions, I believe we have been in such an entrenched mindset that we have lost our perspective. Our "TTWWADI's" have overshadowed the outcomes we hope to achieve.

---

Are your TTWWADI's the problem?

---

What is it we really want to accomplish with our behavior systems and strategies? What's the goal? The obvious answer is behavior change, but the road to that goal is bumpy. And unfortunately, as we move toward the goal, it is very easy to veer off course. Ever have that happen to you? Have you ever left the house, knowing exactly where you hoped to end up, only to get completely lost? This occurs with so many well-intentioned schools I visit. If it sounds familiar, you may be able to relate to the following situation I found at an otherwise great elementary school.

## The Island of Misfit Toys

All the variables were in place for success. The faculty was strong. Academic achievement was evident. Behavior problems weren't overwhelming. The staff had a growth mindset and the administrators were competent and supportive. In an attempt to strengthen student behaviors, the school had just embraced a new philosophy: PBIS, or Positive

Behavioral Interventions and Supports. Based on the founding work of George Sugai and others, this initiative was not a program, but rather a framework for analyzing and strengthening systems the school had in place to support positive behaviors. Having worked with PBIS efforts in schools for a number of years, I was (and still am) a huge fan of this body of work. "They are headed in the right direction," I thought to myself.

As part of the initiative, the faculty implemented a "Caught You Being Good" system. When students were "caught" making good choices, they received golden tickets that would be placed in a fishbowl in the office. Every Friday, tickets were randomly selected and the good choices of these students would be highlighted during the morning announcements. The students also received a certificate to take home to their parents.

In an attempt to turn things around for students who had significant behavior problems, staff members were encouraged to seek them out, increasing their chance to receive tickets. As a result, there were a disproportionate number of the behaviorally struggling students positively acknowledged over the loudspeaker each week.

To end the semester, the school's behavior committee held a pep rally celebrating students from each grade level who had received many golden tickets. High school cheerleaders and the drumline were invited to be part of the event. The celebration started with a high school student talking about the importance of good behavior. He ended his talk very pointedly, *"The following students at this school exemplify great character, as evidenced by the frequent good choices they make."* One by one, students from each grade level were called to the stage, encouraged by the drummers and cheerleaders. By the time the last of the twenty-five students made it to the front, the elephant in the room was abundantly clear to both staff and students. The stage was almost solely comprised of students who had the most extreme behaviors. The gathering looked like "The Island of Misfit Toys." Meanwhile, the students who naturally embodied the best character on a regular basis sat in the audience perplexed. At this point, I thought to myself, "something is wrong with this picture."

Clearly, no one set out for this to happen. The committee had good intentions but, somehow, had experienced a system failure. The staff became so engrossed in "catching kids being good" and rewarding the positive behaviors of one group of students, that they completely lost their way. It's easy to get lost if we don't keep our eyes focused on the outcomes we hope to achieve.

## What are Our Ultimate Outcomes?

It's hard to judge the *success* of our efforts if we don't articulate the desired *outcomes*. Behavior change comprises many variables and it is important to tease them out so we are able to evaluate current practices, as well as those we hope to eventually implement. Each of these outcomes contributes to a child's behavior in some meaningful way.

## Fixed or Growth Mindset - Are You Being Good?

*"Was he good today?"* is a common phrase parents ask teachers when they pick up their children from school. The problem with this type of question is that behaviors are rarely completely good or completely bad. Rather than seeing behavior as black and white, it would be more constructive to view behaviors as a complex series of grey tones with differing levels of intensity. Yet some systems and strategies have outcome-based rewards and punishments that inadvertently create a fixed mindset of right and wrong, or good and bad. The students who adhere to the standard and receive the desired rewards are the *"good"* kids, and those who don't are the *"bad"* ones.

In reality, I believe behaviors lie on a continuum. There are no "good" and "bad" kids. There are simply varying degrees of skill development and, accordingly, different behavioral choices students can make along that developmental continuum. Wouldn't we prefer to help our children view behavior change as an ongoing process? By acknowledging that they all have strengths

Dan says...

*There are no "good" and "bad" kids. There are simply varying degrees of skill development*

and deficits, we can help them improve their skills, no matter where they fall on the continuum.

Do we want students to view behavior in static terms of good and bad…or to see behavior as a learned skill – a process of *continual improvement*?

### Focus of Attention – Look What He's Doing!

When systems or strategies have built-in punishments and rewards, those are the *outcomes on which* students often fixate. I would hope our goal is for students to focus their *behavioral choices* and put forth continual effort, rather than obsessing over a prize. The focus of our attention should be on the *process* of behavior change, more so than the *product* of the associated positive or negative consequence.

In addition, many strategies garner a great deal of public attention with students focusing on other children's behaviors: *"Michael moved his clip today."* Not only does this reinforce the "good/bad" kid mentality, it also can serve to draw more attention to the very behaviors we are trying to extinguish. With some systems, both at home and in school, students often focus on and report the behavior of others to adults: *"Kendra didn't get to go to the party because she didn't have enough behavior tickets."*

*On several occasions I was surprised to learn how many parents knew about behavior problems occurring in my class. Then I realized some students were going home and giving their parents a breakdown of which kids had received which consequences. I didn't like how my students were getting a bad reputation because the parents were only hearing the negative.* – L. Mendenhall

By having students focus on the *process* of developing skills rather than the *product* of rewards or punishments, we empower them to focus on their own choices as a means of strengthening their own behaviors.

> Do we want students to focus on the outcomes of *rewards* and *punishments* or their *ongoing behavioral choices*?

### Motivation - What's In It For Me?

*"If you have a good day with the substitute tomorrow, you will get more marbles in the jar. You know what that will mean – when the jar is filled, we have a class party."* At first glance, this line of thinking seems reasonable – make good choices and good things will happen. However, if we think about the motivation behind the behavior, a concern arises. Do we want students to have a good day with the

*If we want students to do the right thing because it's the right thing to do, we have to ask ourselves if our strategies are working for or against us.*

substitute teacher to get marbles? Or do we want them to make good choices because we should treat guests with respect? If we want students to do the right thing because it's the right thing to do, we have to ask ourselves if our strategies are working for or against us. Most strategies and programs focus on providing external consequences and rewards as the motivation for good behavior. However, I believe when a great deal of emphasis is placed on external reinforcements, be they positive or negative, we run the risk of doing so at the cost of internal motivation.

Watch what happens when a kindergarten child falls and gets hurt: "*Mrs. Applegate, can I take Jake to the nurse?*" The first inclination is not, "*Mrs. Applegate, can I take Jake to the nurse so I can get a sticker?*" Empathy is naturally present in young children; we just have to do our best to nurture it, rather than providing incentives that overshadow it.

Do we want children to behave so they receive an *external reward* OR because they have an *internal motivation* to do the right thing…simply because it is the right thing to do?

## Locus of Control – It's All Your Fault!

At one point in my early parenting years, I had quite an "aha" moment. My son was in fourth grade, which was a period of great power struggles between us. One day after school, he hadn't been home long before my frustration level with his behavior ramped up, and I sent him to his room. When my wife got home she asked him why he was there. *"Your husband sent me here,"* he told her, implying that if she had married someone else he might not be in his room. That was the point at which I realized he did not see any connection between his *behavior* and the *consequence*. All he could understand was that he was in his room because of me. It was *my* fault rather than a consequence of *his* behavioral choices. We all want some semblance of control in our lives. The problem with many behavior systems is that they rely on an external locus of control to affect change. In other words, the teacher is in control of the outcome:

*"If **you** don't get busy, **I** will have to sign your folder."*

*"**I'm** about to give out tickets to students who have their agendas signed."*

If we want children to take responsibility for their actions, the language and systems we use need to provide them the opportunity to make independent choices. Adults are not always around to direct behaviors, so allowing younger children to make choices independent of adult directives provides them opportunity to learn from their mistakes when the consequences are not as life-altering.

> Do we want children to act in an *independent manner* (Internal Regulation) or to be *dependent* on adults to control outcomes (External Regulation)?

## Relationships – Do I Care?

When examining behaviors, it is important to analyze the context of the relationships involved. Does the behavior system or strategy serve to strengthen or tax the relationships? When children succeed because of an intervention, relationships can be strengthened, but when they are always in trouble, those relationships can suffer. If a student is continually in trouble, the child/teacher relationship becomes strained, the parent might begin questioning the teacher's motives, and the parent's disappointment and frustration can begin to erode the bonds between parents, child, and teacher. I experienced this with Micah. When he continually got in trouble for getting "minus" marks in his folder, our relationship became stressed. I have since learned that when relationships are taxed due to a system or strategy, it is a red flag that the system or strategy needs to be reexamined. Conversely, when children succeed within a system of interventions, those relationships are often strengthened.

> Do our strategies strengthen or tax teacher, student, and parent *relationships*?

## Effectiveness – Is This System Working?

The ultimate yardstick for any system should be the effectiveness of the effort. Put another way: Does the system work? Is behavior change evident? There are many factors to consider in order to answer this question. Although many systems do change behavior, we must look further to determine if we are experiencing short-term compliance-based responses or actual long-term behavior change. These are two different outcomes; the latter of which is difficult to assess. A student on a tracking sheet might do a great job holding it together in short bursts to get a reward or avoid a consequence. However, this does not necessarily mean the positive behaviors will be sustained after the rewards and punishments have been taken away.

> Do our strategies yield improvement in *long-term behavior*?

## Hope and Effort – What's the Point?

Success breeds success. When our efforts pay off, we are encouraged to work harder, but when what we are doing isn't working, discouragement sets in. This discouragement can lead to implosion (withdrawal) or explosion (acting out behaviors), neither of which are productive responses. If systems or strategies are not yielding positive results, self-esteem begins to drop over time, and the child often stops trying. Teachers frequently see this at test time, with comments like "Mr. Roberts, I'm not going to pass the test. What's the point?" If a child doesn't see hope of succeeding, they may give up, at which time, no amount of intervention will yield productive outcomes.

> **Dan says…**
>
> *If a child doesn't see hope of succeeding, they may give up, at which time, no amount of intervention will yield productive outcomes.*

Does the student see hope for success? Put forth good effort?

## Don't Throw Out the Baby with the Bathwater

When evaluating our current practices, we can't just look at the system or strategy. We have to look beyond the strategy and examine *how* it is being used. For example, once teachers at our school began to abandon their use of the clip system, one teacher approached me and told me she liked the system and had no plans to abandon it. As we talked, it became apparent that the *way* she implemented the system was quite different from the norm. Listed below are some of the key differences:

| Traditional Use of the System | How She Implemented the System |
|---|---|
| All students had clips on the chart. | Only a few students had clips, as the others were successful without it. |
| All students had the same behavioral standards. | The students using the chart set individually targeted goals. |
| The class clip chart was posted on the wall. | A small individual chart was kept at each child's desk. |
| Students moved their clips when directed to do so by the teacher. | Students reflected on their behavior at set intervals and moved their own clips through self-evaluation. |
| At the end of each day, before leaving, the teacher moved all clips back to green. | At the end of each day, the teacher conferenced with individual students using the system, discussed progress, and set goals for the following day. |

Based on *how* she implemented this system, it both aligned with the school's philosophy and yielded positive outcomes in the areas noted above. Again, the *system is not always the problem*. The problem is often found in how the system is being implemented. Our goal is not to throw the baby out with the bathwater, as the old saying goes. If something is working, we want to continue its use. However, we must do a better job of analyzing our practices to make certain they are moving us toward the outcomes we hope to achieve.

## Abandon Ship

As the urban legend goes, when the captain of a naval vessel discovered he was on a collision course with what appeared to be another vessel, he radioed ahead and requested the oncoming ship to change course. He soon received a response denying the request. The captain sent a second, more emphatic message, which indicated his superior rank, and once again advised a change in course. Soon after, he received a second response: "I'm only a seaman second class, but I recommend you be the one to adjust course." At this point, the captain was livid, so he fired back an order indicating he would not back down. As captain, he commanded the seaman to alter his path. "Stay your course if you'd like, but I'm not going anywhere," responded the seaman, "I'm a lighthouse."

And with those three words, the captain's entire perspective shifted.

I believe sometimes, like the captain of that vessel, we get so focused on the "TTWWADIs," that we fail to see how our practices are working against our desired goals. Just as the captain of the naval vessel had to adjust his perspective and alter his course, I challenge you to continue reading and do the same. I'm confident the result for you will be worth the journey.

CHAPTER FOUR

# Shifting Our Perspective

> *If you don't like something, change it.*
> *If you can't change it, change your attitude.*
>
> – MAYA ANGELO

**"Can you give our teachers more tools for their toolbox?"** It's one of the most frequent questions administrators pose to me. *"Our teachers are really struggling and need some ideas about how to contain all these behaviors. Do you have a good workshop for that?"* Although I definitely understand the request, this type of approach makes me twitch. Yes, I can provide numerous behavior strategies, but rarely is lack of strategy the real problem. When it comes to behavior interventions, we have to look beyond the strategies themselves and uncover the belief system upon which they are grounded - for that is often where true change needs to occur.

## Help Needed

In the span of three days, I visited about twenty different classrooms in one particular school. My job was to observe teachers, provide strategies as appropriate, and report the outcomes back to the administrators. As it was explained to me, the teachers in this school were divided into two groups: those who had good behavior management skills, and those who didn't. From the beginning, I was told which teachers fell into which categories. The administrator said the *"good"* teachers handled discipline problems in their classrooms and rarely referred students to the office. But, the teachers he was most concerned about had poor management skills, as evidenced by loud transitions, noisy classrooms, and more frequent office referrals.

My time in the school was quite eye-opening, as I was young and inexperienced in my role as a consultant. Prior to visiting the classes, I had made a nice matrix for feedback and was prepared to make notes of both "gems" (areas of strength), and "opportunities" (areas for improvement). My observations in the classrooms uncovered both...just not in a way I had anticipated.

When I sat down to discuss my finding with the administrator, his first question raised a red flag: "Were you able to give the teachers some good tools for their toolbox?" My response was instant, "There is no right answer to the wrong question."

## Differing Beliefs, Differing Outcomes

The teachers did fall into two categories, just not the ones the administrator had identified. The majority of the identified "good" teachers did have strong behavior management interventions; yet, they appeared to be based in the context of fear. These teachers expected silence while working, and listening during lectures. You could hear a pin drop in these classrooms. It seemed to me the students behaved because they did not want to get in trouble. They also seemed hesitant to volunteer information or take part in discussions. The teachers ran punitive classrooms, based in a "because I said so" mindset.

Meanwhile, many of the teachers who were noted for having poor management skills appeared to foster healthier behavioral climates. It appeared these teachers worked to build relationships with the students as the primary means of providing boundaries. Their styles seemed less punitive, but also less restrictive. Students talked and interacted more freely, and the classroom operated in a democratic, rather than autocratic, style. This is not to say there weren't behavior issues evident in some of these classes, but those behavior issues concerned me less than the broader issue of conflicting belief systems feeding the practices of the teachers in this school.

The teachers I visited seemed to have very different belief systems feeding their discipline styles, which was why problems were evident school-wide. *Do we want good behavior based on external compliance or on internal self-regulation? Do we use punishments as the primary means of shaping behavior or do we use teachable moments?* We can't address the specific strategies for accomplishing our goals until we clearly identify the belief systems on which the strategies are based. And shaping belief systems is a much more complicated process than merely providing teachers with a few "tools for their toolbox."

## Different Experiences, Different Realities

Our experiences contribute to our beliefs. Our beliefs contribute to our behaviors. Of course, teachers see this play out in the classroom with many students who have challenging behaviors. Take Josiah, for example. On the

Dan says...

*Our experiences contribute to our beliefs. Our beliefs contribute to our behaviors.*

surface, Josiah was defiant (meaning he clearly did not follow directions). He also could be oppositional (meaning he usually did the opposite of whatever was requested of him). If you said, *"please, sit down,"* he would stand. If you said, *"no,"* he would say *"yes."* You get the picture. Although these overt behaviors were not appropriate, it is important to examine the beliefs and experiences that shaped them, in order to get a better understanding of the forces at work.

Josiah lived with his single mom, and as mom indicated, dad was never involved. A neighborhood friend watched Josiah after school because his mom usually worked late into the evenings. Josiah's schedule was erratic because mom's work schedule changed weekly. Josiah's mom knew he had behavior problems, but she did not trust the school system. As mom explained, she had been put in the *"dumb"* classes when she was young and was worried the same thing would happen to her son. She also believed Josiah was often targeted as the *"bad"* kid. Mom was clearly concerned she would get fired if the school called her at work *"one more time."* She felt Josiah acted out in order to get to see her. She spanked him,

This is a puzzling picture to piece together. Josiah's outlook began with mom because *her experience of failure* in the school system shaped *his belief* that school was an unsafe and untrustworthy place. These beliefs triggered her own oppositional *behaviors* against the school, which in turn strengthened her negative *experience* with school. This cycle continued to spiral and, generationally, was now trickling down to her son.

Josiah was *experiencing* a world in which he had little control. He wanted to know about his dad and to see more of his mom. He craved a consistent schedule and routine, which his family life didn't provide. He was continuously in trouble at home and was often placed in time out at school. His *beliefs*, we could assume, were that both home and school were unsafe places, as evidenced by his ongoing punishments. His oppositional *behaviors* were likely an attempt to gain some semblance of control over his life. Josiah reacted to this lack of control with oppositional and defiant behaviors.

Dan says...

*The first step in changing behavior is to understand where it comes from.*

Though Josiah's behaviors weren't acceptable, they were certainly understandable. The first step in changing behavior is to understand where it comes from. If experiences shape our beliefs, which in turn shape our behaviors, then it is easy to see why so many educators are struggling with classroom behaviors in today's society. The problem starts with the disconnect between *our* experiences and the experiences of our students.

## "Because I Said So. That's Why."

I'm guessing it will surprise no one who knows me that I got in trouble in school for talking too much. My punishment? I had to write lines: "*I will not talk in class. I will not talk in class.*" I remember having to fill up an entire page, single-spaced, and then turn it over to keep writing. And since my handwriting was abysmal, I vaguely recall having to start over and "do it again, *neatly.*"

As mentioned earlier, I grew up in a generation of compliance, as did many of my teacher friends. I did what I was told, and the consequence for not doing so was punishment. This sounds much more primitive and archaic than it truly was. The bottom line is that it worked. I understood boundaries, and punishment was effective in stopping my misbehavior. *My experiences of punishments* shaped my *belief system of compliance*, which in turn, shaped my *behavioral interventions* as both a parent and a teacher. Even today, my gut-level reaction is to punish children when they are not compliant.

The problem, as noted in the first chapter, is that the punishments used on me "back in the day" don't work nearly as well as they did when I was young.

In the last twenty-five years, assertive discipline practices have become less and less effective. The result? Our experiences with punishment didn't seem to be working, so the pendulum began to swing towards attempting to reward behaviors, instead.

## Stickers, Smellies, Warm Fuzzies – Just Say "No"

I was very excited to read a story with an eager group of kindergarten students. It was the first time I had had the opportunity to in my new school, so I picked just the right book and made the story as interactive as possible. I was a blast. The kids seemed to enjoy the book and the whole experience felt like a huge success. However, the second I set the book down, I had a class full of students waving their fists in the air. The teacher quickly informed me I was supposed to give each child a sticker if they had behaved: *"Do you not have any? I can give you some,"* she kindly offered.

Something didn't feel right in that moment. I read. They paid attention. They enjoyed the story. I enjoyed the story. Why would we complicate this natural ebb and flow moment with stickers? Shouldn't the normal consequence of paying attention be the enjoyment of the story and a happy feeling in our hearts? Or did we create an expectation of reward by always giving out stickers? And if so, did the stickers shift the students' focus to one of behaving, just to get a reward?

The moment was made even more awkward when I looked down and saw three boys sitting in front of me without their fists in the air, looking sad and dejected. *"They don't want a sticker?"* I asked. *"Oh honey, they gave up on getting stickers a long time ago,"* replied the teacher. I immediately thought of my son, Micah. Something is most definitely wrong when I have three five-year-old children giving up hope within the first nine weeks of school. What a long twelve years of schooling they had ahead of them!

Don't get me wrong; I'm an advocate for teacher's noticing good choices and reinforcing positive behaviors. However, there is a difference between *acknowledging* and tangibly *rewarding*. When we constantly offer rewards for appropriate behaviors, we run the risk of inadvertently creating a belief system of expectation. Are these really the *experiences* we want to provide our students? I believe, in an attempt to positively shape behaviors using rewards and punishments, we have unintentionally created *belief systems* that work against our goal of students doing the right thing just because it's the right thing to do.

Dan says…

*When we constantly offer rewards for appropriate behaviors, we run the risk of inadvertently creating a belief system of expectation.*

*I never really gave out tons of stickers to students, but when I did, the students started to expect them. Plus, some students seemed to do what I asked, just for the reward. Since I've mostly gotten away from giving them, the students don't even ask about them anymore.*

– H. Ballew

## Distorting Our Kid's Beliefs

In preparation for writing this book, I did informal research, which was very enlightening. I asked random students a few questions:

| | |
|---|---|
| **Me:** | *Why is it important to walk and not run in the halls?* |
| **Student:** | *If you run, you'll get in trouble.* |
| **Me:** | *Why is it important to be quiet when you are doing your work?* |
| **Student:** | *I'll get a mark in my behavior folder.* |
| **Me:** | *Why should we not shove someone (at recess) when we get angry?* |
| **Student:** | *You'll have to sit out.* |
| **Me:** | *Why should we sit with our hands in our laps?* |
| **Student:** | *We will get a sticker on our chart.* |

These were not the answers I was hoping for. Do I really want the student's focus to be on the external avoidance of punishment, and an expectation of reward? Or would I prefer the internally motivated altruism? These are the kinds of answers I was *really* hoping for:

| | |
|---|---|
| **Me:** | *Why is it important to walk and not run in the halls?* |
| **Student:** | *If you run, you could fall and hurt yourself or someone else.* |
| **Me:** | *Why is it important to be quiet when you are doing your work?* |
| **Student:** | *When I'm quiet, I am being considerate of others.* |
| **Me:** | *Why should we not shove someone (at recess) when we get angry?* |
| **Student:** | *It's not safe. We can use our words to express feelings instead.* |
| **Me:** | *Why should we sit with our hands in our lap?* |
| **Student:** | *If our hands are on the carpet, someone might trip or step on them.* |

See the problem? The *experience* of punishment and rewards is shaping and distorting their *belief* of why they should work to make good choices. In an attempt to alleviate the problem of poor behaviors, we inadvertent shift the student's focus toward external factors of avoidance and expectation.

Some teachers might argue, *"Well, I wouldn't go to work if I weren't paid. What's wrong with rewarding good behavior?"* The problem, as I see it, is that it works against our long-range goals of what we want for children. Do we really want them to become adults who simply go to work to get paid, or would we prefer them to focus on doing what they love, while still acknowledging the reality and necessity of pay? Using a school analogy: Do we want students to behave in the cafeteria so they don't get in trouble, or because they understand that doing so shows respect for others?

Aside from internal and external motivation, we also need to understand the reality: adults won't always be around to reward and punish. If we design a system based on external motivation, what will happen when we are not around to enforce it?

**Dan says...**

*Aside from internal and external motivation, we also need to understand the reality: adults won't always be around to reward and punish.*

We should work to make certain our practices shape healthy beliefs that align with the long-range goals for our students. This is why more "tools" or strategies won't fix the problem, as the problem is usually not about strategy, but beliefs. As illustrated below, our strategies are just the tip of the iceberg.

**Behaviors/Practices**

**Beliefs/Principles**

## It All Starts With Our Beliefs

*"He's going to make it into the gifted program. He's incredibly smart."* This was a phrase I heard often from one of my colleagues. In fact, she said it about a good majority of her students. To her credit, she was a strong teacher. She, like all teachers, had her own gifts and challenges. But she was known for her strong *belief* in the intelligence of her students - even when the students did not believe in it themselves. This is why it came as no surprise to me that many of her students <u>did</u> qualify for the gifted program in our school. Her *belief* actually influenced their successful outcomes.

**Dan says...**

*This is what I want for all teachers: for our positive beliefs about our kids' behaviors to influence their successful outcomes.*

This is what I want for all teachers: for our positive *beliefs* about our kids' behaviors to influence their successful outcomes. Our beliefs need to move our students forward and propel them toward better behavior, even when they don't believe in themselves. If we believe student behaviors *will* improve, our strategies are more likely to be successful. Once we align our beliefs with the outcomes we hope to achieve, we are ready to discuss specific strategies for building a foundation of good behavior in our students.

CHAPTER FIVE

# BUilding the FOUndation

**School was challenging for me** when I was younger. Although my mother regularly assured me I was quite intelligent, my grades and classroom performance often indicated otherwise. Many concepts that came naturally to my classmates were difficult for me. When I am asked today about my own school experiences, I can't provide many details. For my own sanity, I think I blocked out that period in my life.

I do, however, remember Mrs. Zamora's English class. I loved it. English wasn't my strongest subject, but it didn't matter. I connected with Mrs. Zamora, who believed in me. It was her power of belief that convinced me to join the speech and drama club, an area in which I excelled. To this day, I remember placing first in humorous interpretation at a speech tournament in New Orleans. As I was walked back to my seat after receiving the trophy, she smiled and said, *"I told you you'd be good at this."* Funny, I don't remember much of the content of her class, but I still remember the positive emotional connection. With regard to my school experience, the climate she created in her class was a game changer in my life.

## It All Starts with the Climate.

Walk into any room and you can get a feel for the climate without anyone saying a word. It's the first assessment in every classroom observation I make, as I know the emotional climate has a strong impact on behavior. You can tell if the students are happy, engaged, or embarrassed. And these emotions often provide a window into understanding their outward behaviors.

Have you ever heard a song and immediately felt transported back to prom or some other significant event from your past? The experience is a result of an anchor - a connection in the brain. The song was originally anchored or attached to the memories of the event itself. Anchors can have both positive and negative feelings attached to them, which is why it is so important for teachers to create positive classroom climates that will translate into healthy school associations. Students who have positive school experiences carry these anchors into future classrooms. If our goal is to promote positive student behaviors, we must first examine all the factors affecting the classroom climate; so healthy anchors can be established.

**Safety – Run Away**

A healthy classroom atmosphere starts with all students feeling physically and emotionally safe. If this basic need is not met, the concern will often manifest through students' behaviors. Safety is at the base of Maslow's Hierarchy for a reason; our brains are survival-oriented. When a threat is perceived, behavior problems often escalate and new learning ceases. Although we understand this on a common sense level, our classrooms are not always run in a way that addresses this need.

When I worked as a teacher in a behavior unit, I saw how fear, hunger, and lack of sleep contributed to my students feeling unsafe. As a result, they often acted out. This was especially evident when my students visited other classrooms with behavior tracking systems. *"Mr. St. Romain, if I get a mark in my folder, my dad's gonna kill me!"* Although this is a common figure of speech, I knew many of my students really did not feel as though their homes were safe places. The behavior folder systems used in our general education classrooms only contributed to this problem.

**Strategies that Promote Feelings of Safety:**

- ☛ To the extent possible, help students get basic needs met (sleep, food, etc.).
- ☛ Provide structure in the classroom.
- ☛ Acknowledge and validate students' feelings.
- ☛ Build individual relationships with students so they feel comfortable coming to you with problems.

**Structure – I Need Routine.**

Have you ever had your morning routine interrupted? How's your mood and behavior when you don't have your regularly scheduled cup of coffee? When we have structure in our lives, we are able to predict. And when we are able to predict, we feel safe. Remember that word safety? Healthy routines promote feelings of safety. And when routines are interrupted, behaviors often escalate. Many students experience this phenomenon when there is a substitute teacher in the classroom. The novelty of having a new person in charge can completely disrupt the existing daily routine and amplify negative behaviors in the process.

**Strategies that Promote Good Classroom Structure:**

- ☛ Have a strong classroom schedule - and follow it.
- ☛ Teach classroom procedures (lining up, requesting attention, etc.).

- Identify behavioral expectations and discuss potential natural and logical consequences when students fall short of them.
- Practice expected behaviors regularly so they become habits.

## Belonging – I Need To Connect.

We don't have to look any further than incidents of school shootings to understand the importance of *belonging* when it comes to a healthy classroom culture. The common element among the majority of perpetrators in these cases has been isolation. They isolated themselves from the larger community, lacking a sense of belonging. When a child does not feel as though he or she belongs, alienation sets in. Classroom practices that foster a sense of belonging vary, but all are designed with the goal of helping individuals connect to the larger community.

## Strategies that Foster a Sense of Belonging:

- Hold morning meetings and circle time. Both of these practices allow the class to come together and discuss issues important to both students and the teacher.
- Incorporate partnering activities and group projects to help build student-to-student relationships.
- Encourage family participation to strengthen the overall sense of belonging in the community.

- Develop classroom rituals. This might be something as simple as having students stack chairs at the end of the day, or greeting each other when entering the class each morning.

**Teacher-Student Relationship – The Power of a Person**

I was faced with some very severe behaviors when I started teaching, but I was not prepared to work with such an oppositional fifth- grader. Nicci was a mess - a good mess - but a mess, all the same. I tried intervention after intervention, but found little success when it came to changing her defiant behaviors. Our interactions usually turned into power struggles, followed by her having physical outbursts, which usually required restraint for safety reasons.

Luckily, there was Mrs. Ruff, another teacher in the same hall. She could walk into my room at any time, look at Nicci and say, *"get off the floor."* At which point Nicci would stand up, say *"yes ma'am,"* and sit down quietly in her chair. It drove me crazy that Nicci listened to Mrs. Ruff, but not to me. This pattern went on for weeks until one day after school Mrs. Ruff came to my classroom. *"Why won't Nicci listen to me?"* I asked. Just as calmly as she could, Mrs. Ruff looked me straight in the eyes and said, *"Dan, no matter how bad you may want to, you will never be a middle-aged black woman. It's just not going to happen."*

I will never forget that conversation. Mrs. Ruff went on to explain that Nicci listened to her because of their shared cultural experience. That was their connection. Although it wasn't something I could share, Mrs. Ruff told me my job was to find a different way to connect with her so that I too could make a difference in her life. Mrs. Ruff had the power with that little girl. She was the one person who could strongly impact Nicci's behavior because she was the person with the relationship. Although I envied the fact that Nicci listened to her, I realized that if I hoped to have the same power, I too would have to find a way to connect with her. If we want to have a healthy class climate, we must foster healthy relationships - for that is where the power truly resides.

**Strategies that Foster Healthy Teacher-Student Relationships:**

- Greet students by name at the door each morning.
- Get to know student interests and incorporate them into the classroom.
- Redirect students in private when possible.
- Spend individual time with students; it's hard to build a relationship in a group setting.

*I find when I get a child alone, away from friends; I can usually get to the root of the behavior problems. One-on-one time also really helps me build relationships, which I think motivates my students to try harder. I know that's what it does for me!*

– M. Cook

## Teacher Affect – The Power of a Presence

Have you ever known people who put you at ease with their presence? The teachers' *affect*, as evidenced by their body language, facial expressions, attitude, and tone of voice, all contribute to the climate, as these factors set the emotional tone for the classroom community. For some teachers this comes naturally. They are highly requested by parents and are often given many students with behavior concerns, due to their success in working with them. I find these teachers usually have some commonalities that center around their affect: They use a quiet voice and are able to model calm behaviors. They have a voice tone that is neutral, rather than escalating. In addition, they convey safety and security with their facial expressions. These teachers' power is in their ability to create a welcoming classroom environment with their positive presence.

### Strategies that Foster Healthy Teacher Affect:

- Reflect on personal qualities that influence the class climate. (What message does my tone of voice send? How's my volume? etc.)
- Have a fellow teacher observe you, and share observations about your affect.
- Set a goal to improve your affect in one specific outlined area.
- Video yourself presenting a lesson and view it critically. We have a difficult time understanding our own affect and how it comes across to others until we can see it.

## Control – The Power of Balance

*"Good teachers never lose control,"* or so the adage goes. However, there is a difference between gaining control of a situation and being controlling. Control is an issue of balance. We all need order in our classroom, and that requires us to maintain control. If we are unable to interrupt disruptive behaviors, the atmosphere in our classroom will suffer. When students don't sense we are able to keep order, their anxiety increases, and anxiety will always escalate behavior. Conversely, if we are too controlling we create a different set of problems.

High degrees of control invite power struggles, especially with students who have oppositional behaviors. This issue plays out regularly in classrooms, with teachers trying to maintain order by exerting control. I speak from experience on this one. I routinely had "last word" battles with one of my sons, and of course, the issue was control. My son needed to feel some control in his life, but I had a very hard time giving it to him. I took his oppositional behaviors as a sign of disrespect. My wife had to help me "step away" on many occasions. *"Sometimes you have to lose the battle to win the war,"* she often reminded me.

Although a high level of control might be effective in extinguishing inappropriate behaviors, it can create a tense learning environment, with students afraid of taking risks. A teacher once told me, *"Come see my class. I don't have behavior problems. My kids know not to step out of line."* Upon observing her class, I discovered this was true. But I also didn't see this as a good thing. I find when students are given opportunities to make choices and exercise self-control, they are less likely to exert control in unhealthy behavioral ways, disrupting the class environment.

### Strategies that Foster a Healthy Sense of Student Control:

- Give students a limited range of choices. "Would you prefer to sit with the group or by yourself?"
- Assign students classroom jobs. Jobs give students a means of contributing to the class, which helps with purpose and connectedness.
- Allow students time to talk and interact without fear of getting in trouble.
- Involve the students in developing expectations and targeting goals for improvement.

### Engagement – The Power of Attention

**Dan says...**

*A positive class climate is built on positive emotions. Learning should be an enjoyable process.*

A positive class climate is built on positive emotions. Learning should be an enjoyable process. That doesn't mean it will always be easy or fun. By the same token, it shouldn't be a grueling experience. We want students to be engaged in interesting and meaningful learning, so our lessons should reflect that. Attention wanes when students become disengaged. I've heard the phrase "A *bored dog is a bad dog*," on more than one occasion. Not to compare children with animals, but students who are not engaged often contribute to poor behaviors and classroom disruptions.

"Hot Potato" was one of my favorite review techniques, but my students had many others. We reviewed vocabulary by passing around index cards with words on the front and definitions on the back. We practiced multiplication facts by jumping on floor mats, and studied science terms with fly swatters and posters. Engaging activities go a long way in contributing to a healthy climate in the classroom.

**Strategies that Boost Engagement:**

- ☛ Mix things up! Start classes with review activities that get kids up and moving.
- ☛ Find out the interests of your students and infuse them into lessons.
- ☛ Take a project-based approach to student assessment. Have students write and act out commercials "selling" a concept, or write a song demonstrating something they have learned.
- ☛ Change up the environment. Let students sit on the floor, in different desks, or better yet – head outside for a lesson. Fresh air and a change of scenery can do wonders for waking students up and plugging them back in to learning when they are tired.

# Be that Teacher

I envy my wife. She teaches fifth grade, and if home is any indication of the climate she establishes in her classroom, her kids are lucky. In twenty-five years of marriage, I've never heard her raise her voice. *I don't think that's natural, but I appreciate it all the same.* She is quiet, soft-spoken, and for the most part, rarely gets outwardly flustered. She has an uncanny ability to set people at ease, as she's good at building relationships and making individual connections with kids. I know this, because on Halloween, she regularly has former students knocking on our door to say "hi." She gets it. She understands the important role climate plays as a foundation for learning and good behavior.

I hope every person can recall a teacher who created a healthy classroom climate. When you entered the class, you felt a sense of belonging, safety, comfort, and engagement. **Be that teacher**, because once you connect with your students and create a positive climate, then the true work of behavioral instruction can begin.

*"Your wife was my teacher in 4th grade. She was so awesome. I believe if I had had more teachers like her, I would have become something to be proud of.*

*It's probably been 18 years since she was my teacher, but I remember her the most. She would get me to write. I know for sure if middle and high school had had teachers who tried like she did, I would have gotten through school."*

– A former student of my wife's sent this to me on Facebook.

CHAPTER SIX

# Teaching Skills

**The goal was to find a secretary for my boss.** I was on a committee with four other people and we narrowed down the search to two women, both in their forties, who sat out of the workforce for a while to focus on raising their children. The first candidate had an impressive resume with a great deal of training that would be an asset in the job. Although she was talkative to a fault, and seemed somewhat brusque, she had experience with databases, worked with Excel spreadsheets and knew her way around the computer. The other candidate was lacking in technical areas, but all of us agreed she had great communication skills and was a very likeable person. They both had strengths and challenges. We struggled so much with the selection that our boss decided to interview both candidates herself. The committee members were curious to see which of the two she would hire.

Our boss looked perplexed after the interviews because she felt the decision was quite obvious. As she explained, *"She might not pick it up easily, but I can send my secretary to get training on databases, spreadsheets, and computer skills – even at forty years old. Teaching communication and people skills at that age is immeasurably harder."* She had a point, of course - one we had not considered.

## Windows of Opportunity

The brain is an amazing organ. It grows, learns, and readily adapts. It's malleable. This is especially true for younger individuals. However, as we age, the brain becomes less pliable. We are still able to learn new information, but some tasks become more difficult. This is especially the case in regards to altering existing behavioral patterns.

Have you ever tried to teach a coworker social skills? How did that work? As we get older, our behaviors develop into ingrained pathways in the brain, otherwise known as habits. Some of our habits are good and some are not. And once a habit is formed, breaking it is a challenge. This is why it is critical to focus on developing good patterns of behavior in our students while they are young. When they are older, breaking those habits becomes a far more daunting challenge.

## "Wanna Play?"

"Blind Man's Bluff" was a painful game for me. I played it a lot with friends and siblings when I was young. As I recall, the person who was "it" was blindfolded and spun around until quite dizzy. Then they would have to find and tag another player. All the while, the other players are calling out and throwing objects at the poor unfortunate blindfolded person. We usually played in the bedroom where, invariably, an entire mattress would be flung in my direction. I received many a bruise during that game. Nevertheless, when I played childhood games like that one, I learned very important life skills:

- **Listening** – I had to rely on my sense of hearing when blindfolded.
- **Being Quiet** – When I made noise, I was quickly tagged.
- **Putting Forth Effort** – The harder I tried, the better I got at playing the game.
- **Accepting Disappointment** – Somebody always has to be "it."
- **How to Treat Others** – When I targeted players, they would target me on their turns.
- **Natural Consequences** – If I was being obnoxious, no one wanted to play with me.

Games taught me how to manage my emotional state, interact with others appropriately, and make good choices based on what I knew to be right and wrong.

As the influence of technology grows stronger, many children today spend less time playing and interacting with others, and more time in front of screens. With students spending less time practicing social interaction outside the school setting, I believe it is important we spend more time teaching behavioral skills in our classrooms. Unfortunately, many of us assume the children who enter our classroom know how to behave socially. These days, it is probably safer to assume children have no prior behavioral knowledge. This insures that nothing is left to chance, and we can be more purposeful about teaching behavioral skills, just as we do other cognitive ones.

> **Dan says…**
>
> *As the influence of technology grows stronger, many children today spend less time playing and interacting with others, and more time in front of screens.*

## The Big Picture

How do we purposefully teach behaviors? We start by focusing on three overarching categories of development:

**Emotional:** Our ability to inhibit or exhibit our feelings appropriately

**Social**: Our ability to interact with others in a suitable manner

**Ethical:** Our ability to understand right from wrong, and make choices accordingly

From birth to about age five, young children are self-centered. This is normal. Their survival instinct is to focus on their own wants and needs, often at the expense of anyone within earshot. *(Have you ever been seated next to an unhappy toddler on a plane?)* For this reason, **emotional regulation** should be one of the first skills we develop in young children. Helping them manage their own feelings appropriately will strengthen their ability to interact with others in a healthy way.

As children get older, usually around age five, **social awareness** kicks in. Though they may still focus on their own needs, they do so in relation to others, through comments like, *"Are you going to come to my birthday party?"* or *"Mrs. Bates, Michael is not supposed to be here! The boys haven't lined up yet."* At this age, children are trying to navigate integrating self with others, which is why teaching social skills at this point is so critical.

**Ethical development** unfolds over the course of several decades. Although young children have the ability to understand concepts of right and wrong, the frontal lobes in the brain don't fully develop until the mid-twenties. Moral judgment, and cause and effect are processed in these frontal lobes. (*For parents with teenagers, this explains a lot.*)

When children are young, they should receive a great deal of instruction in all three of these areas to strengthen positive behaviors. In schools, however, *cognitive* achievement takes center stage, which means efforts to reinforce behavior in these three areas is often less systematic and purposeful. If we are going to change this equation, a good first step is working with students to establish clear boundaries through rules and expectations.

## What Do You Want From Me?

When I visited a third grade classroom, I talked with a number of students about their classroom expectations. When I got blank looks, I knew I needed to change my question. *"What are your classroom rules?"* I asked. *"Listen to the teacher,"* said one. *"They're up here,"* said another, pointing to a pre-made laminated poster from the local education shop hanging on the wall. *"What does it say?"* I asked. *"Hold on,"* she said as she walked closer to read it. The last student I asked looked at me, shrugged, and walked off. At that moment, I thought, *"Houston, we have a problem."* It's impossible to enforce

**Dan says...**

*There are two types of boundaries that need to be established in the classroom:* **rules** *and* **expectations**.

behavior expectations if students don't know what those expectations are.

There are two types of boundaries that need to be established in the classroom: **rules** and **expectations**. If we are going to align our language with our beliefs, it is important to understand the difference between the two, and how they are both used.

*Rules* are put in place for safety and should be non-negotiable. When a rule is broken, there should be a consequence that is consistently enforced. Rules are best reserved for "big ticket" safety issues: fighting, weapons, vandalism, etc. It is also important to clearly articulate why rules are in place and to help students understand the specific consequences for not adhering to them.

**An example of a rule:**

No Fighting. We solve problems through *discussion*, not *aggression*.

**An example of a consequence if that rule is broken:**

If a student fights, the student must leave that setting immediately to cool down. Before re-entering the class, the student must work through the problem with the teacher. Home will be notified, as this is an issue of safety.

*Expectations* are agreed upon behavioral standards. Often established collaboratively, expectations outline our desired behaviors for a given setting. We treat classroom expectations as we would goals. They are behaviors we strive for, but understand that our students may fall short in meeting them. Consequences for not adhering to expectations come in the form of teachable moments and agreed upon courses of action.

**An example of kindergarten expectations:**

- We use our listening ears.
- We use our walking feet.
- We keep our hands, feet, and objects to ourselves.
- We follow directions right away.

In my observation, one of the most common rules in many classrooms is: *follow directions*. Since rules should be non-negotiable points of discussion, it is better to frame following directions as an expectation rather than a rule. Otherwise, students should receive consequences each time a directive is not followed. Given the sheer number of directions a teacher provides in a given period, this becomes difficult to consistently enforce.

Many teachers and schools frame their expectations in broad terms:

- Be respectful.
- Be responsible.
- Be safe.
- Be kind.

I would note these are better termed *philosophies* or *principles*, as they are umbrella concepts that are both subjective and vague. Having said this, it is fine to use these as expectations, as long as the terms are clearly defined with specific desired behaviors. For example:

**An example of fifth grade expectations:**

- We respect others (*principle*) by working quietly(*expectation*).
- We show responsibility (*principle*) by bringing our agenda to class every day (*expectation*).
- We stay safe (principle) by keeping our hands to ourselves (*expectation*).
- We show kindness to others (*principle*) by being inclusive when working in groups (*expectation*).

# Keep it Simple

With regard to **rules** and **expectations**, I recommend teachers have expectations for the classroom, and allow the school's code of conduct to outline the rules. By doing so, we accomplish several things:

- By clearly outlining our rules and expectations we are able to distinguish between non-negotiable safety issues and behavioral skills that need ongoing teachable moments.
- By defining desired behaviors as expectations we reinforce the message that behavior falls on a continuum. Rather than focusing on the end result of being right or wrong, we frame

behavior as a series of choices and work towards continual improvement. Expectations are something we strive to accomplish, but understand we may fall short of, at times.

↪ Expectations convey opportunities to improve skills, which is more in line with a growth mindset, whereas rules often convey a compliance or fixed mindset. The former is more in line with the philosophy we want to guide our practices. No matter how good a student is at an expectation, there is always room for improvement.

Teachers may need to outline individual rules for protection of property, etc., but I believe the majority of desired behaviors are better enforced as expectations.

## Focus on the Expectations – Not the Consequences

Some models advocate for clearly outlining and posting consequences, both positive and negative, when students adhere or don't adhere to behavioral expectations. Although I think we should post expectations, I don't believe posting consequences is a good practice for several reasons:

↪ When we have outlined positive and negative consequences, teachers are put in a position of having to continuously evaluate students' behaviors and enforce the associated consequences. This is a challenging task to do *consistently*.

↪ Posting expectations without outlined specific consequences keeps the focus on the behavioral expectations themselves, rather than the associated reward or punishment.

↪ By not posting the consequences, teachers are able to better differentiate the consequences, based on the needs of the child, and choose those that might best accomplish the goal of improving desired behaviors.

↪ Posting consequences also increases the likelihood other students will police the expectations and focus on the behavior of others, rather than focusing on their own behaviors. This is especially the case with younger children: *"Mrs. Weatherston, Felix did not push in his chair. He owes you a ticket."*

↪ With regard to expectations, the practice of outlining positive and negative consequences sits in a mindset of good/bad and right/wrong. If we believe behavior moves along a sliding scale of grey tones, it's not helpful to outline choices in fixed terms of black and white. *

* This is not the case with rules, which should clearly outline specific non-negotiable behaviors. Since rules are outlined for safety, students should understand the pre-determined consequences for not adhering to them.

This does not mean teachers and students shouldn't collaboratively discuss consequences for actions. This practice is very important, but it should happen in the context of ongoing discussions and teaching efforts, i.e., *"Cheryl, what might happen if you don't finish your work now?"* The reflective process of discussing outcomes can be a very strong intervention, helping students learn about the cause and effect nature of their choices. However, when concerns arise, the focus of our efforts should be on teaching replacement behaviors, not on punishing and rewarding, which often happens when consequences for expectations are posted.

## Other Considerations When Outlining Expectations

- ↩ Less is more.
  *The more expectations we have, the harder they are to enforce.*
- ↩ Keep them simple.
  *The simpler they are, the easier they are to remember.*
- ↩ Focus on desired behaviors.
  *Emphasize the specific desired behaviors rather than ones to avoid ("Walk in the halls." vs. "Don't run!").*
- ↩ Develop expectations with the students.
  *If you outline the expectations with your students, they will be more likely to take ownership and remember them. This collaborative process will lay the foundation for many teachable moments in the future.*
- ↩ Have students memorize expectations (this can be fun when expectations are put to a chant or song!)

*The goal is for the expectations to become second nature to the students. This is best accomplished if students memorize and internalize them. However, if students have to refer to the expectations on a sign or poster, it is unlikely they will follow them.*

↪ Consider connecting the expectations to specific social skills that students will need as adults; remembering our goal is not about their success just in school, but in life.

## Consistent Skills / Consistent Language

When articulating rules and expectations it is critical to use consistent language. Students are more apt to both understand and adhere to outlined expectations when adults use consistent language. By hearing consistent language from multiple staff members in many settings, students are better able to understand and internalize expectations.

*I never realized how important focusing on the same skills, using the same consistent language was in helping with my discipline efforts. I found when I had a common language, students better understood my expectations, and they could communicate the expectations with each other, as well.*

– L. Everett

In reviewing various behavior and counseling programs, the term *social skills* is often used as a generic overarching term encompassing social, emotional, and ethical areas of development. For clarity and consistency of language, I believe it is better to use the broad term of *behavioral skills* when referring to all three. Each of the three can be broken out to help parents and educators better understand the specific areas of development. For example:

- *"Michael has clear strengths when it comes to social skills (interacting with others); however, we are still working on helping him verbalize when he is angry rather than storming out of the room." (emotional self-regulation)*
- *"I can always trust Tasha to walk directly back to class independently without running (good ethical choice), but when she is walking back with other students, she really struggles with keeping her hands to herself." (social skills)*

## Pick a Skill – Any Skill

If you search the term *"social skill"* on the Internet you will discover an infinite number of behavioral skills that can be taught. Although all the skills are important to some degree, I recommend choosing a set number on which to focus. By doing so, we are able to provide a deeper level of instruction around each.

Once you've chosen the skills, develop consistent definitions or teachable phrases for each. When social skills are described in vague terms and inconsistent ways, the skills are not as easily internalized. Promote consistent language by using repetitive phrases that reinforce the specific expectations. Repetition strengthens teaching efforts. Also, consider having students call words back to you, completing different phrases to promote greater involvement and ownership in learning.

Listed below are some of the common skills I practice with students, along with the wording I use to teach them:

| | |
|---|---|
| **Following Directions** | We follow directions right away. A teacher's job is to keep you safe and help you learn. |
| **Paying Attention** | We pay attention with our eyes and ears. Where the eyes go, the brain follows. |
| **Being a Good Friend** | Good friends are inclusive. Good friends use kind words. Good friends take thoughtful actions. |
| **Respecting Personal Space** | We keep our hands, feet, and objects to ourselves. I have my space. You have your space. |
| **Getting Attention Appropriately** | When I want the teacher's attention, I raise my hand. Just because we think it, doesn't mean we should say it. |

| | |
|---|---|
| **Accepting Disappointment Appropriately** | We get what we need, but we don't always get what we want.<br><br>We use our words to express our feelings. |
| **Putting Forth Good Effort** | We use our time wisely. We do our work precisely.<br><br>The more we practice, the better we get. |
| ***** **Taking Responsibility for Our Actions** | We tell the truth.<br><br>We take ownership for our choices. |
| ***** **Making Good Independent Choices** *or*<br><br>**Resisting Peer Pressure**<br>**(For Older Students)** | We make choices with our brains.<br><br>Do the right thing. |

* The last two skills can be challenging for younger children, given their developmental age. This does not mean we avoid teaching the skills, but it is important to understand children may not fully grasp these skills until they are older.

## Proactive Teaching Efforts

At the school where I work, I visit classrooms every two weeks to teach behavioral lessons. I usually read a book and introduce a specific skill. In between my lessons, the classroom teachers focus on the targeted skill through examples. Over the course of the school year this allows us to provide roughly eight lessons in the fall and ten in the spring. When deciding on how to introduce and proactively teach behavioral skills, consider the following:

### ☞ Daily Use
The power in this model is not in the initial teaching of the lesson, but the daily reinforcement of the skill. Our goal is for the skills and phrases to become habitual, which is most likely to happen through daily use. Counselors might introduce a lesson, but the reinforcement of the skill is the daily responsibility of the classroom teacher. If this does not happen, the skills are not likely to be remembered or internalized.

### ☞ Ongoing Review
Each time a new lesson is introduced, continuously revisit and reinforce concepts previously taught. The more students practice the language and review old lessons, the better the skills will lock into their long-term memory. I am always amazed at how well students retain the lessons we teach. At the end of the year, I am able to quiz students on all eighteen lessons with close to 100% recall. This is the power of continual review.

### ☞ Make Lessons Meaningful through Experience
Consider ways to augment the lessons using specific activities and experiences. For example: when working on the skill of accepting disappointment, have an art activity and assign students different mediums to use

(colored pencils or markers). Invariably, some students will not get the medium they want, which will allow for a teachable moment on accepting disappointment.

### ↶ Keep Parents in the Information Loop

Work collaboratively with parents to strengthen your efforts. On days when you introduce skills, send notes home so that parents are aware of the skills and language they can be use to reinforce the concepts at home.

### ↶ Have a Guest Teacher

The novelty of having a different person teach skills increases the chance students will better retain the concepts learned. Make it a practice to invite a parent or another teacher to visit your class and introduce skills. One way to do this is to swap classes for behavior lessons with a fellow teacher over the course of a school year. This can be most effective when crossing grade levels, as the novelty factor is stronger. For example, if Mrs. Whiteley's fourth grade students are peer buddies in Mrs. Frierson's first grade class, those two teachers could swap classes for a twenty-minute lesson every two weeks to introduce a specific skill. This strategy affords both teachers the perspective of working with students at a different developmental level, while also providing them fresh insight on their own students from the visiting teacher.

**↩ Work as a Team for Greater Impact**

As with any skill, consistency is key. Although one teacher may successfully teach a specific skill, the impact is greater when all the teachers of a grade level or school are using the same language and phrases for reinforcement. Consider working as a team to strengthen the overall impact of the effort.

# From Teaching to Targeting

We lay a strong foundation for meeting the behavioral needs of our students when we outline rules and expectations, and purposefully teach those skills using consistent language. This is a great start, but some students will need additional support. Some students will require a more individualized approach that moves beyond the one-size-fits-all method. This is where many systems fall short. They fail to consider the individual differences of our students. If our goal is to help *all* students succeed behaviorally, we must take into consideration their unique skill deficits, while building on their inherent strengths.

CHAPTER SEVEN

# Identifying Gifts and Challenges

> *I only got a seventh grade education,*
> *but I have a doctorate in funk.*
>
> – JAMES BROWN

## Gifted and Challenged

Okay, so I did get in trouble for talking a lot in school. I had what you would call "blurtitis." (Truth be told, this is still a problem for me.) Thoughts passed quickly through my brain and popped out of my mouth before I could stop them. I've always known listening was a challenge for me. Talking? That came easily. My teachers told me I needed to work harder to be quiet, and as far as I can remember, I tried.

This theme of *trying* also spilled over into my academic success, or lack thereof. When I was in school, I spent a great deal of time reading passages and answering comprehension questions. Unfortunately for me, by the time I got to the questions, I had forgotten what I read and had to go back and start over. As this was a common type of assessment, I struggled in school and got pretty mediocre grades. I was told continuously by my teachers to "just try harder." I was never quite sure what that meant. Would it help if I held the books closer to my face when I read?

To make things worse, my slightly older sister was a straight "A" student who attended a summer program for gifted children. This is not to say she didn't work hard to earn her good grades, but learning came more easily for her than me. My mother assured me that my sister and I had the same intelligence, and I just needed to apply myself. I appreciated the vote of confidence, but did not feel gifted in the least. If anything, I felt inferior and disabled in the school setting.

Thankfully, my mother also supported my love for music, which was something that made sense to me. I enjoyed singing and visibly twitched if someone next to me sang the slightest bit sharp or flat. "*Can you not hear that?*" I would think to myself. I also learned how to play the piano rather easily. If I wasn't figuring out a familiar tune, I was trying to write one. This is probably the reason I spent so much time at the keyboard, because in some small way, music helped me feel gifted. And I needed that experience to balance out my feelings of disability at school.

This would also explain why, to this day, I have a visceral response to gifted and talented programs. No matter how much I try to adjust my perspective, deep down I believe all individuals are gifted - just in different ways. Unfortunately,

Dan says...

*I believe all individuals are gifted – just in different ways.*

in the educational system, we view cognitive intelligence very narrowly. I'm convinced the line we create, separating the gifted from the non-gifted, does a disservice to all our children. Forgive my soapbox, but as I lay out my recommendations, it is important to understand my experiences and how they shaped my beliefs regarding behavior.

Just as our gifted programs categorize students as gifted and non-gifted, I believe many behavior management programs create categories of "good" and "bad" students as identified through rewards and punishments. Adults might not intend these results, but all children know that the students who regularly get their folders signed and clips moved, or who sit out of activities, are the "bad" ones. They also know that the children who receive the most rewards are the *"good"* ones. I strongly feel these systems move us in the wrong direction, with regard to both the mindsets we are trying to shape and the strategies we choose to implement. Behavior, like intelligence, falls on a continuum. All children have varying gifts and challenges. It is the teacher's job to help children identify their gifts and challenges, and to differentiate instructional strategies accordingly.

## Differentiated Discipline

If you have ever heard the term *differentiated instruction*, you know it is an important instructional strategy for supporting the individual academic needs of students. However, before a teacher differentiates instruction in the classroom, all students are exposed to the same core content through whole class lessons and group assignments. This ensures all students have the same foundational knowledge. The same should hold true for our behavioral efforts, as outlined in the last chapter. We first develop rules and expectations, using specific skills and consistent language, so our students have a common understanding and vocabulary. Once this is established, we can begin to differentiate behavioral instruction based on the needs of our students.

## That's Not Fair!

When I lived in Chicago back in the late 80's, you could buy just about anything on the streets of the south side. Every morning, as I walked from the elevated train station to the school where I worked, I met some very eccentric vendors trying to sell everything from lamps to clothes. One day a teacher friend of mine purchased ten pairs of the exact same shoe from one of those vendors.

When his students walked into class that morning he handed each of them a pair of the shoes. Rather than hearing *"thank you"* from the students, he got the same response from each: *"Man, I can't wear these."* *"Why?"* he asked. *"Well, first, they're ugly,"* they laughed. *"And second, they won't fit."* Smiling, my friend said, *"But I can't give you all different sized shoes. That just wouldn't be fair."* They looked at him, a bit confused, until the light bulb went off. Fair doesn't necessarily mean one-size-fits-all.

*"That's not fair! How come he gets to use the computer?"*

*"That doesn't seem fair. You didn't give me extra time to do my work."*

*"That's not fair. How come she gets to go first?"*

"Fair," as we know, does not mean we all get the same thing. This is a critical lesson, and one my colleague hoped to drive home to his students by giving them all the exact same pair of shoes. "Fair" means getting what we need to do well. In a truly fair learning environment, strategies are differentiated according to each student's needs. This is the case with both cognitive instruction and discipline. Differentiating discipline starts with identifying students' gifts and challenges, so that individual needs can be determined accordingly.

# We're All in this Together

I usually introduce the concept of strengths and challenges with a two-part lesson. First, I read a book highlighting a person's struggle with mastering a skill of some type. We then discuss all the feelings that accompany the struggle: anger, sadness, and fear of failure. The goal is to help my students identify with the experience and connect to the struggle. I follow this activity by sharing my own struggles in school and the frustration I experienced when my friends picked up concepts easily. In the second part of the lesson, usually on the following day, I read a book highlighting someone with a special talent or skill. We discuss all the feelings associated with success: pride, happiness, relief, and joy. I then share a skill that came rather easily for me. We talk about our gifts and also circle back around to our challenges. When choosing books for this activity, I try to find one highlighting a behavioral example (following directions, paying attention, etc.) and the other, a non-behavioral example (a sport or school subject).

Throughout the week that follows, students spend time identifying their own strengths and challenges in a T-chart or flipbook:

| School Skills that Come Easily to Me | School Skills that are Challenging for Me |
|---|---|
| Writing | Math Word Problems |
| Putting Forth Good Effort | Spelling |
| Handwriting | Respecting Personal Space |

After students have completed this activity, they share their examples with classmates. By reframing all challenges as *skills to be practiced*, I hope students will see behavior as they would any other academic skill: one that can be improved with support and effort. I also circle back to this activity later by having students set goals, which allows us to build on the idea of growth mindset.

In addition to identifying behavior as a skill, having students outline their individual strengths and challenges is a great way to level the playing field in the classroom. Rather than seeing some students as "good" and others "bad," classmates are taught that all individuals have obstacles to overcome, just as they all have gifts to celebrate. This lesson helps reinforce important principles of inclusion, understanding, and empathy.

> **Dan says…**
> *Rather than seeing some students as "good" and others "bad," classmates are taught that all individuals have obstacles to overcome, just as they all have gifts to celebrate.*

## "Shhh…" Unspoken Behavior Taboos

Too often, when a student has a behavioral meltdown in class, the incident is never discussed as a group. In an attempt to keep confidentiality, we often avoid discussing the behavior problems of individual students with the class. Behavior is often considered a taboo subject. We can change this norm by shifting the culture of the class to identify behavior as a skill and build a community of support through open discussion. For example, *"John Marshall was really upset when he left the class. Raise your hand if you've gotten that upset before. I have. Remember, that's something he is working on – using his words when he gets frustrated. Let's talk about things we can do to help him when he gets that angry."* By discussing the incident, we remove the taboo and normalize the behavior, while also acknowledging the feelings and concerns of the class. Discussions also encourage empathy and empower students, enlisting them as partners to help a member of the class community find success.

> *Having students in my class work as a community to help other students break bad habits is so powerful! The students really try to help each other in ways I would never imagine. And it usually only takes one student with an outstretched, accepting hand to start the effort.*
>
> – J. Bonewell

## Reframing Attention

When students draw attention to the negative behaviors of others, it's a good practice to balance the scales by bringing attention to those student's strengths.

**Student:** *"Caleb is putting his hands on the bulletin board when we walk in the halls."*

**Teacher:** *"It's good we all have strengths to balance out our challenges. What did Caleb tell us are his strengths?"*

Another way to handle the situation is through acknowledgement, followed by redirection:

**Teacher:** *"Yes. Caleb did say he has a hard time keeping his hands to himself. That's something he is working on. What's something that is a challenge for you?"*

This helps encourage the trait of empathy rather than judgment.

## Individual Goals

Rather than using a whole-class behavioral system of rewards and punishments, consider having each student choose a goal from a set list of behavioral skills, making certain there are appropriate choices for all students:

- ↪ Respecting Personal Space
- ↪ Paying Attention
- ↪ Putting Forth Best Effort
- ↪ Being a Good Friend
- ↪ Making Good Choices

Once students have chosen their individual goals, find specific ways to keep them focused on those goals. Too often, behavioral goals are treated like New Year's resolutions. We do well the first few days after the goals are set, but once the novelty wears off, our goals are forgotten. Though activities might need to be modified, given the grade and developmental level of your students, here are some simple ways to keep students focused on their goals:

- Post the goals around the classroom and encourage students to support classmates in meeting them.
- Have older students journal each week, outlining specific examples of how they met or fell short of their goals.
- Set a specific time each week for the students to assess their own progress and adjust goals, if needed.
- At the end of the grading period, conference with each student and collaboratively decide on grades or evaluation marks. With this activity, I often find students grade themselves more harshly than their teachers do.
- Have students write periodic notes to their parents about their progress on the goals.

## Daily Behavioral Communication – Just say "No"

Parents can support our efforts in the home setting, but it is important we don't inadvertently damage relationships by sending home daily communication about behavioral progress. Ongoing daily feedback from the teacher can lead parents into seeing behavior as good or bad, rather than focusing on their child's continual growth and improvement.

*"But I have to send home a daily note about behavior. Parents expect it."*

Yes, parent communication is important, but we don't provide daily communication about any core academic subject, so why should we treat behavior differently? Changing behavior takes time and when parents receive daily feedback from us, they can easily lose sight of the long-range goal, and begin to focus on day-to-day student choices. If behavior doesn't improve quickly, most parents feel the need to respond by using punishment or rewards. *"If you have three good days, we can go get pizza."* This is exactly the type of mindset and strategy we want to discourage.

> Dan says…
>
> *Changing behavior takes time and when parents receive daily feedback from us, they can easily lose sight of the long-range goal, and begin to focus on day-to-day student choices.*

If parents are accustomed to receiving daily behavioral communication, you will need to explain to them the reasoning behind your new methods. Here is an example of what you can send home:

Dear Parents,

I hope you had a great summer with your child. We have had a great start to our school year and now, as we settle into a consistent routine, we are ready to dive into specific targeted areas of instruction. This year we will be targeting student behavioral skills just as we do academics.

During these first few weeks, I have introduced students to our classroom expectations. By now, the children are familiar with these expectations and, for the most part, are successful in following them. Now we can work to individualize support and help the students identify both their strengths and areas of concern.

This week, after reviewing our classroom expectations, I will meet with each of the students individually to set one behavioral goal. Rather than monitoring a daily folder or tracking with a system, I will help the students monitor their own behaviors. I want your child to follow the expectations of the class because it is the right thing to do, not to avoid punishment, such as negative marks in a folder. Once I meet with your child, we will work together to inform you of the chosen goal.

Although you will not receive a daily grade or note, you will receive intermittent feedback from me on how your child is progressing. This will allow you to talk with your child and provide encouragement from the home setting. Please note: Although you won't receive daily feedback, we will let you know when we see really great progress or when strong concerns arise.

As I set goals with your child, I welcome your input! If there is a goal you would like for us to consider, or if you have any questions or concerns, please feel free to contact me. As always, I appreciate your support from home. I am looking forward to a productive and fun-filled year with your child.

Sincerely,

*Your Child's Teacher*

*When I told my parents we would no longer have daily behavior communication, most were relieved. I told them I knew they had a lot going on in their own lives, so I wanted to relieve them of the worry of having to check folders each night. Once they saw the benefits, they fully embraced the change.*

– P. Young

## Parent Communication Recommendations:

- ↪ Less is more. Let parents know you will inform them when really great things happen or when really concerning things happen, but everything else will be lumped under day-to-day teaching, which you will handle in class.

- ↪ Using communication folders is fine; but make certain the folders are about communicating *all* information and not just focusing on day-to-day behavioral choices.

- ↪ We often tell children not to tattle, so I try to model this expectation, as well. When possible, use communication as a tool to acknowledge good choices, rather than poor ones. This builds trust with the student and encourages the parent.

- ↪ Involve your students in the process of communicating with parents. Help them reflect on and evaluate their own behaviors. When possible, have children mark their own folders and even write their own notes home to their parents.

- When it becomes necessary to inform parents about behavior issues, have the student be responsible for that communication. When we let parents know about behavior problems, we take away the natural consequence of the student having to do so. You can still talk with the parents and coach them on how best to handle the situation. I tell parents, "Please don't bring up this incident. My goal is for your child to tell you what happened and take ownership for his or her choices."

- Calls are always preferable to sending emails or notes home. Calls allow you to convey emotional context that may be lost in written communication.

- If you receive an email from a parent and sense that he or she is frustrated, don't respond with specific content. Validate the communication and suggest a call: "Thank you for bringing this to my attention. Is it convenient for me to call you after school so we can talk?"

- When tension is mounting or a parent is angry, request a face-to-face meeting. This strategy allows the parent time to calm down and gain some perspective, before discussing the issue.

*I found my parents sometimes really misunderstood my notes home, but this didn't happen when I called home. Calls allowed me to build trust with my parents, and once that happened, they were able to hear anything I had to say.*

– K. McCulloch

# The Mason Report

If I needed any evidence of the benefits of targeting skills and setting individual goals, Mason certainly provided it. Mason was typical of students with severe behavior problems. He was in first grade and his biggest struggle was keeping his hands to himself. His mother asked to meet at the end of the second week of school. She let me know she was very discouraged, because she was receiving daily calls from the school about his behavior. I was sad to hear about his struggles, but hopeful; Mason loved his teacher, seemed to be making friends, and enjoyed coming to school each day. I provided some suggestions and asked her to keep me updated on progress.

Two weeks later I received another call from Mason's mother and the news was not good. Mom had started volunteering in the classroom so she could get a better feel for how things were going, but she quickly noticed a disturbing pattern. Every time she entered the room, at least one or two students gave her the "Mason Report":

*"Mason had to turn his card twice yesterday."*

*"Mason grabbed my jacket in line."*

Mom was very upset because she knew her son was getting the *"bad kid"* label. Mom admitted that Mason fit the description, but she hated to see it happening. She knew the other students meant well, but was discouraged all the same. *"The worst part,"* his mom said, *"is that Mason's affect is changing. He isn't nearly as happy when he gets up in the morning. And twice, he has asked if he could just stay home from school."* Mason's mother didn't know what to do. She was concerned about Mason's behavior and his relationship with the other students in the class.

When I saw Mason's teacher after I met with his mom, she too, was worried that Mason was being ostracized. She wanted to do something to help her students be more understanding of his behaviors. This seemed the perfect time for me to present a social skill lesson to her students. I talked with the students about a boy whose challenge was needing to use a wheelchair to get around. After a discussion about gifts and challenges, the students all identified their own challenges, as well as their gifts, and set goals for themselves. We also talked about ways we could support each other in meeting those goals. There is a happy conclusion to this story. About a month later, I had a visit from Mason's mother. She had just left the classroom, where she got the "Mason Report," but this time it had a different slant:

> *"Mason is getting better at keeping*
> *his hands to himself."*

> *"Mason is doing a little better. He only*
> *hit me once this morning."*

Mom was elated. Although she acknowledged his behavioral progress seemed slow, she was pleased to see the huge change in the other students' attitudes towards her son. Mason was being accepted as part of the class community. And that was a great start.

## Overcoming Our Challenges

Mason had difficultly keeping his hands to himself. But like all of us, he had strengths in other areas. As we have seen in this chapter, our goal should be to build on our students' strengths, while helping them overcome their challenges. Mason's teacher tried to teach him how to keep his hands to himself, but he still struggled with how to demonstrate that skill consistently. As with any skill, what Mason really needed was more time to adopt the desired behavior through practice.

CHAPTER EIGHT

# Practicing Skills

> *An ounce of practice is worth more*
> *than tons of preaching.*
>
> – MAHATMA GANDHI

## The More We Practice...

My wife taught fourth grade for the majority of her career, and her favorite subject was writing. On any given night, I could usually find her downstairs perched on a chair, shirt over her legs, grading writing samples. Occasionally, she would burst into gleeful laughter at her students' natural talent. She also had many students who struggled with writing. In these instances, she would coach, conference, inspire and motivate, all the while having her students continually *practice*.

For some students, progress was made with just a few tweaks, but for others, the process was grueling. It seemed to be two steps forward and one step back. She never gave up, and if a student ended the year without mastering a skill, she felt confident knowing she had added to their knowledge base. She also understood that it was a cumulative effort. Teachers before her, and those after, would all add to that student's skillset.

This, of course, was the emphasis of the last chapter. We teach behavior just as we would any other subject. When a student struggles, we coach, conference, inspire, and motivate. Notice I didn't say *punish*? If a student can't write a coherent paragraph, we don't resort to punishment, just as we wouldn't if he couldn't tie his shoes. We don't punish students for skill deficits; we *teach*. And when a student is weak in a skill area, the best way to improve is through practice. I tell the students, *"My job is to teach you important skills. The more we practice, the better you will get. Let's practice."*

**Dan says...**

*We don't punish students for skill deficits; we teach.*

My oldest son handed me a bow tie during his first year of college. *"How do you tie this?"* he asked. Since I had no experience with this fashion accessory, he suggested we solve the problem the way he did most often. *"The internet!"* he exclaimed. He was right. There were numerous step-by-step tutorials to walk us through the process. Being a college-educated person with an advanced degree, I expected to pick up the skill rather easily. This was not the case. Don't get me wrong - I could tie it just fine. The problem was the end result. My bow tie looked like it was broken, tilting to the left or right, too big on one side, or too small on the other. In a word, it looked *off*. Being the tenacious type - determined, driven, and prideful, I could not let the bow tie win. I wore bow ties exclusively for quite some time, until slowly, they began to look less mangled. Now, several years later, I have moved to the pinnacle level of bow tying. I can tie them perfectly without even thinking – and it is all thanks to the simple strategy of *practice*.

## Committing "Assumicide"

Shifting our perspective from a model of punishment to practice can be a challenge for some educators, due to their fixed mindset. Teachers often tell me, *"Dan, his behavior is not the result of a skill deficit. That student knows exactly what he is doing; he is just making a bad choice."* I find this broad assumption can lead to problems. Choice is one factor, but many other issues could be influencing the behavior as well:

- The student knows what they are supposed to do, but in the moment their behaviors are ruled by her emotional state, which could be silliness, anger, lack of sleep, etc.

- The student operates on "autopilot." Ingrained habits of inappropriate behavior take over when they are not really concentrating.
- TThe student doesn't know what is expected of them. This is either because expectations are not clearly spelled out, or adults send mixed messages about expectations by inconsistently enforcing them.
- In times of crisis, the student regresses to younger, less skillful behaviors as a means of coping.
- Fear of embarrassment or failure takes precedent over demonstrating the expected behavior.

## Warning...

Once you begin viewing discipline as a chance to strengthen a deficit skill, your current interventions will begin to seem inappropriate and somewhat absurd. Take, for example, two students who have a problem with arguing or pushing on the playground. A typical response to this behavior is to separate the students or have them sit out of recess. When thinking about this situation from a skill standpoint, we should ask ourselves this question:

> How will separating the students or having them sit out of recess teach them how to work cooperatively through the conflict?

Removing the potential for conflict stops the immediate problem, but does nothing to teach the long-term skill. At best, we are probably only delaying the problem until the next time they interact. If anything, their behavior indicates a need to be paired together *more* often so they are able to learn how to work cooperatively. This is the mindset of skill development.

Listed below are specific examples of ways to use discipline as an opportunity to teach, rather than relying on punishment to change behaviors:

| Concern | Consequences Designed as an Opportunity to Teach a Skill | Consequences Designed as a Punishment |
|---|---|---|
| A student makes a hurtful comment to another student. | The student comes up with three kind or helpful things to say to that student. | The student receives a negative mark in his or her folder. |
| Two students argue in a learning center. | Although the students might need to be separated initially to deescalate the situation, the students are paired together more often, allowing them opportunities to work through their problems. | The students are separated and put in different learning centers. |

| | | |
|---|---|---|
| A student continually bangs on the computer keyboard. | The student is allowed to work on the computer only at select times when an adult is available to monitor. As the student demonstrates improved behavior without direct supervision, he or she is given more independent computer time. | The student is not allowed to work on computers for a specified period of time. |
| A student runs around the cafeteria during lunch. | The student sits at a supervised table with lunchroom monitors providing frequent reminders about appropriate behaviors. | The student has to eat in the office. |
| Several students don't pay attention during a whole-class reading time. | The students are pulled together in small groups to practice appropriate behaviors associated with paying attention. | The students miss out on fun activities, while getting a lecture about the importance of paying attention. |
| A student does not follow directions. | The student is given multiple opportunities to both practice and demonstrate the skill. | The student is placed in time-out. |

Be prepared for the responses you will invariably receive from some students: *"Mr. Matthews, I know what I'm supposed to do. I don't need to practice."* In these situations, let the student know, *"Just because you know what you are supposed to do, doesn't mean you've developed the skill into a good habit. That takes time and practice."*

One benefit of emphasizing practice over punishment is that it allows you to differentiate discipline interventions based on individual needs and skill deficits. Behavioral choices help you determine what consequences will best strengthen skills.

*Differentiating discipline through practice is easy. The students just work on what they need to work on, which may be different from what other students need. When students are all practicing different skills, they see we all have different strengths and ways we can grow. This approach takes judgment out of the equation and helps reinforce the philosophy of discipline as a teachable moment.*

– M. DiSabato

# Working in Groups

As with academic skills, behavioral skills can be practiced one-on-one, or in a group setting. When determining the frequency and duration of the practice sessions, consider the severity of the deficits, as well as the developmental age of the child. Younger children will usually need more frequent support, but given their attention spans, practice sessions will usually be shorter. Older students might not need the same frequency of practice, but will likely need more in-depth instruction during longer sessions. Student attention spans and behaviors will provide clues as to the best length for each practice session.

| Younger Students | More | Shorter | Less |
|---|---|---|---|
| | ⬇ | ⬇ | ⬇ |
| Older Students | Less | Longer | More |
| | **Session Frequency** | **Session Length** | **Content Depth** |

With younger students, incorporate practice sessions into your lesson plans throughout the day or week. Small group practice that targets critical skills can be very beneficial in developing good behavior habits in young children. The classroom is the most natural setting to learn skills that can then be generalized in a variety of other settings.

### In-Class Small Group Practice Sessions
(Younger Students)

One or two times per week, during a fifteen-minute carpet activity (calendar time, etc.), monitor student behaviors in the following three skill categories:

☛ Following Directions (carrying out directives without multiple prompts)

☛ Paying Attention (sustained eye contact)

☛ Getting Attention Appropriately (raising hand, not calling out)

Immediately following the activity, announce a *practice session*. Students who demonstrated these three skills are released to work quietly on some other activity. The remaining stay back for a few minutes to practice the deficit skills as you read a short story and ask simple comprehension questions. If other students are talking or making noise, this can help the students practice blocking out external distractions.

Emphasize that each student has to practice different skills. No one is in trouble when they have to practice. We practice a skill so we can improve it. We simply practice because the skill has yet to be mastered.

As students get older, the pack usually separates, with many students naturally internalizing positive behaviors while individual students still struggle. As this happens, offering pullout sessions for more intensive support can be beneficial. Pullout sessions are often provided by the counselor, but can also be offered by classroom teachers.

During a set intervention behavioral block, each classroom teacher can choose a specific skill to target, with individual students attending the appropriate sessions needed to address their skill deficits. With this type of support, scheduling issues need to be addressed and grade level teachers must be provided instruction on how best to teach behavioral skills in a small group setting. This is where a counselor can be of great benefit to the staff.

---

**Pullout Group Sessions** (Older Students)

When students are pulled for behavioral skill support, take into consideration the following guidelines:

↪ Focus on a specific social skill for each group. Provide several sessions, with different lesson plans, all on this same skill. This can be challenging, as many programs only provide one lesson for each social skill covered. The programs are designed to teach that one skill, and then move on to another skill during the

---

next group session. When we jump from skill to skill, students do not have time to focus on or internalize each skill. If a student struggles academically, we would choose one targeted area to teach, and then reinforce that one concept over several lessons. Behavior lessons should be no different.

☛ Vary group activities so skills are learned and internalized in a variety of ways:

- Art Projects
- Writing Assignments
- Goal Setting and Evaluating
- Problem Solving
- Reading and Discussing a Book

☛ Pull students based on a targeted skill deficit. When all students in the group are focusing on the same skill, consistency of language and intensive teaching strengthens the likelihood positive behavior change will occur. It is tempting to group students based on scheduling availability rather than on the behavioral needs of the students. Unfortunately, when this is the case, focusing on specific targeted skills becomes a challenge.

☛ Provide a common language and specific instruction on the targeted skill. This information must be shared with all teachers, so that the concepts can be reinforced in multiple settings. The ultimate goal is for the skills learned during the group sessions to be generalized in the classroom setting. In order for this to happen, the teacher must be made aware of the instructional practices occurring during group time.

↪ Use a tracking sheet. The tracking sheet provides a vehicle for the student to analyze their progress with help from a caring adult.

## What's Your Mindset?

A positive growth mindset uses behavior concerns as an opportunity to teach; offering a chance to practice a skill until it becomes a healthy habit. Teachers who have a belief system based in punishment might adopt the *idea* and *wording* of practice, but will still invariably use practice in a punitive way:

↪ "If you don't like practicing, next time you need to make a better choice."

↪ "If you do that again, you are going to owe me some practice time."

Practice is not punishment and should not be used as such. Our body language and tone of voice contribute to the overall message

our students receive. When we practice behavior as we would any other cognitive skill, we are positive, optimistic, and encouraging. By communicating in this way, we increase the likelihood our students will be successful. We also strengthen our relationship with them, encouraging the students to work hard to achieve the desired goals.

It is said, "practice makes perfect." If this is the case, it is an unfortunate one for most students with behavior concerns, as many years of practicing inappropriate behaviors means they have perfected the art of misbehavior. Once poor behaviors become ingrained into habits, retraining the brain and developing new habits becomes the new challenge. The sooner we adopt this positive mindset, the fewer ingrained habits our students will have to break.

 CHAPTER NINE

# Breaking Habits

> *The only proper way to eliminate bad habits is to replace them with good ones.*
>
> – JEROME HINES

**My boys could sense the question** before I even asked it. *"Yes dad, you locked the car door!"* they would say. It's a question I've posed to my family countless times over the years. Truth be told, I don't even ask it anymore. I just quietly step outside and press the key fob, so my brain makes a conscious mental note that the door is locked. That's the problem with ingrained patterns: when we do something repeatedly, the behavior moves from a *conscious response* to an *unconscious reaction*.

As we examine student behaviors, we have to take into consideration the role habits play. Working with younger students has its advantages – their habits are not too deeply entrenched. First grade students have had, at most, only six years to solidify their behaviors. Compared to working with the same behaviors in the later teen years, there is a great deal of hope that the behaviors, no matter how inappropriate, can be reshaped. As students get older, and behaviors become more entrenched, the habits become more challenging to break.

We focus on teaching and practicing behavior skills to lay a strong foundation for children in younger grades. However, once skills have been taught and children understand how to cognitively execute them, the great challenge becomes ingraining those patterns as habits. As one of my sons told me on numerous occasions, *"Dad, I know what I'm supposed to do, but at that moment, doing it is hard."* What he was really saying was, *I know the skill, but I have a bad habit and when I'm not really concentrating, I do what I've always done.*

## How Hard Can it be? Teaching with Attainable & Sustainable Goals

If you have ever tried to break a habit, you know it's about more than just making good choices. There are many contributing factors:

- Past Experiences – *How successful have I been in the past?*
- Hope – *Do I believe I can be successful?*
- Relationships – *Are the people I trust supporting me?*
- Self-Concept – *Do I believe I'm worth it?*
- Resources – *Do I have the emotional energy and time to devote to this?*
- Priorities – *Are other issues diverting my attention from this?*
- Motivation – *Do I want to change enough? Do I care?*

These factors affect success rates, and the more strikes a student has in each area, the harder it is to change behavior. When faced with severe behavioral problems, it's best to start by setting a *specific* goal. We discussed *general* goal setting guidelines in a previous chapter; though, when we are working with a student who has more entrenched behaviors, we have to drill down into more specifics. General goal setting is not enough. We need to be intentional about what goals we target and how we monitor progress:

**Focus On One Goal at a Time**

Students often have many problematic behaviors, but if our goal is to create positive change, it is critical to focus on only one. The brain can only consciously attend to one thing at a time, so when students try to improve several behaviors at once, very little change occurs.

*When I looked at the overall behavior of my students who were struggling, I often felt overwhelmed, defeated, and as if nothing worked. But when I started focusing on one specific goal, things changed. Not only were the students more hopeful, they were more successful, too. I could really see gains and I felt as though we were not always in crisis mode.*

– L. Large

## Start with the Easiest

Involve the student in choosing a goal that is realistic and has the best chance for success. For example, paying attention, is a good expectation, and it can be a good goal, but it must be clearly defined:

- ↪ We pay attention with our eyes, by looking at the speaker.
- ↪ We pay attention with our ears, by staying quiet while we listen.

Since we expect our students to pay attention for long periods of time during the school day, tracking this behavior can be difficult. When we break the school day into smaller, more manageable chunks, and choose a specific time frame to both monitor and track the behavior, we increase the probability of success.

- ↪ Paying attention during transitions
- ↪ Paying attention during whole group carpet time

# The Success Loop

When we choose an easy goal that is very attainable, we allow our students to build on their early successes. This gives a child hope, which is critical. The child who does not see hope for success will give up. And if a child gives up, the behavior will never change. It's a vicious cycle, as evidence by the graphic below:

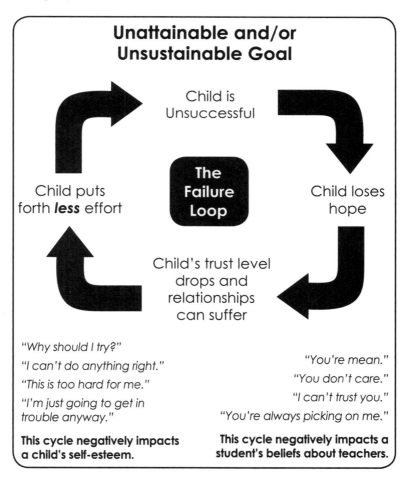

## Unattainable and/or Unsustainable Goal

Child is Unsuccessful

The Failure Loop

Child puts forth *less* effort

Child loses hope

Child's trust level drops and relationships can suffer

*"Why should I try?"*
*"I can't do anything right."*
*"This is too hard for me."*
*"I'm just going to get in trouble anyway."*

**This cycle negatively impacts a child's self-esteem.**

*"You're mean."*
*"You don't care."*
*"I can't trust you."*
*"You're always picking on me."*

**This cycle negatively impacts a student's beliefs about teachers.**

Conversely, by choosing a goal that is attainable, we increase the likelihood the child will get into a loop of success, which is our goal:

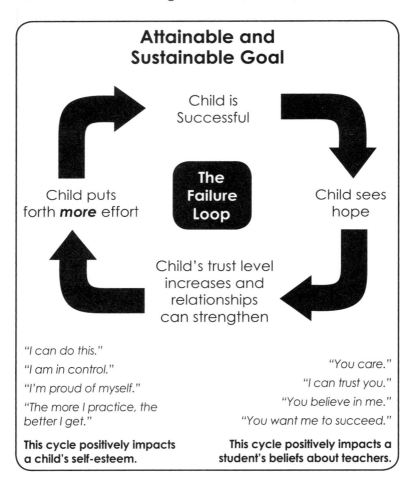

## Attainable and Sustainable Goal

Child is Successful

The Failure Loop

Child puts forth **more** effort

Child sees hope

Child's trust level increases and relationships can strengthen

*"I can do this."*
*"I am in control."*
*"I'm proud of myself."*
*"The more I practice, the better I get."*

**This cycle positively impacts a child's self-esteem.**

*"You care."*
*"I can trust you."*
*"You believe in me."*
*"You want me to succeed."*

**This cycle positively impacts a student's beliefs about teachers.**

## Collaborate and Track Progress

Once a goal is targeted, decide on the best way to monitor the student's progress and meet regularly to discuss it. This is a critical step. We want the child to become more aware of their behavioral patterns through ongoing discussions, and thus be in a better position to change them.

Use a simple tracking sheet to monitor progress and analyze patterns:

## Tracking Sheet Example

Name_____

Dates_____

Goal_____

**+ Met Goal**
**- Keep Trying**

### Monday
___ AM Transition
___ Morning Meeting
___ Math
___ Language Arts
___ Literacy Instruction
___ Recess
___ PE
___ Lunch
___ Science/Social Studies
___ PM Transition

### Thursday
___ AM Transition
___ Morning Meeting
___ Math
___ Language Arts
___ Literacy Instruction
___ Recess
___ PE
___ Lunch
___ Science/Social Studies
___ PM Transition

### Tuesday
___ AM Transition
___ Morning Meeting
___ Math
___ Language Arts
___ Literacy Instruction
___ Recess
___ PE
___ Lunch
___ Science/Social Studies
___ PM Transition

### Friday
___ AM Transition
___ Morning Meeting
___ Math
___ Language Arts
___ Literacy Instruction
___ Recess
___ PE
___ Lunch
___ Science/Social Studies
___ PM Transition

### Wednesday
___ AM Transition
___ Morning Meeting
___ Math
___ Language Arts
___ Literacy Instruction
___ Recess
___ PE
___ Lunch
___ Science/Social Studies
___ PM Transition

### Comments

# Tracking Sheet Tips

↶ Track the progress of the one, established "doable" goal.

↶ Choose the timeframe to monitor behaviors that are most conducive to success. Some students can work for sixty minutes on a goal before it is evaluated. Other students need the evaluation window broken down into smaller chunks of time. As we have discussed, younger children tend to need more frequent feedback due to shorter attention spans.

↶ Work with the child, allowing them the opportunity to evaluate progress. *"What do you think, Michelle? How did you do?"* We are not always going to be around to provide the feedback, so we want to instill practices encouraging self-evaluation and self-regulation.

↶ To the extent possible, avoid connecting successes and failures to punishments and rewards, allowing the goal-setting process to be the focus. *"You're right, Trina. It was a hard day. But think about how you did on Thursday. Remember, it takes time to break habits. You'll have a fresh start tomorrow. Let's set a goal."*

I acknowledge that with students exhibiting more severe behaviors, teachers may choose to use negative consequences and positive incentives to begin the process of changing behaviors. However, to the degree possible:

↶ **Use natural and logical consequences over arbitrary punishments:**
*Rather than telling the students they will lose recess if they get one more bad report from the lunch monitor, have a discussion with them about what they think could be done to fix the problem. Invite the lunch monitor to the class and encourage problem solving. The students might choose to write apology notes to the monitors or self-select to sit in spots in the cafeteria more conducive to better behavior.*

↶ **Use intrinsic, natural, and logical incentives over external tangible rewards:**
*Rather than giving students tickets or school "cash" for appropriate behaviors, highlight the positive outcomes of their good choices. "Nathan, since you finished your work, you have extra time on the computer." "Bella, great job using your words to tell why you are upset. Yes, you may go to the library and switch out your book."*

↶ **Use intermittent reinforcements over scheduled ones:**
Rather than telling the students they can eat outside when they have one week of positive comments from the lunch monitor, leave out the reward and have the class focus solely on the goal of treating the lunch monitors with respect. Intermittently affirm the students' efforts and declare a picnic celebration for the following day. This keeps the focus exclusively on the targeted goal rather than the attached reward.

# How to Handle Behavior Documentation

Tracking behavioral progress can be a challenge and is often a double-edged sword. Documentation is needed in order to evaluate growth, but once you gather a few days of data, it all begins to look the same. You can get to the point where you want to write, "*See yesterday*" or "*ditto*" across the page. Once the data begins to look the same, documentation is treated as a box to be checked or a hurdle we have to jump through in order to get more outside support.

**Dan says...**

*Documentation provides us an opportunity to examine behaviors and look for trends and patterns that might be helpful in determining best strategies.*

The practice of documentation is most effective when it supports a reflective mindset. Documentation provides us an opportunity to examine behaviors and look for trends and patterns that might be helpful in determining best strategies. Documentation also provides insight into which specific skill might best be targeted in goal setting. Ultimately, documentation should be a tool for reflection and data-driven decision making. For example, when a student has many behavior concerns, the data gathered can help you decide on the most effective goal to set.

The process of targeting, monitoring and documenting goals should focus on ongoing teaching efforts and continual improvement around a specific behavior. As with any skill we teach, our role should be one of coaching, encouraging, re-teaching, and providing feedback. Parents can be a huge support in this process, but communication is the key.

## Parent Education and Collaboration

Educating parents on how to best support their child in the behavior change process is important. This is especially the case when we are dealing with more severe behaviors, as parents can inadvertently work against our efforts if left to their own devices. For example, in an attempt to support the school, many parents will use punishment as the primary means of trying to change their child's behavior. Unfortunately, for some children with more severe behaviors, this strategy can exacerbate the very behaviors we are working to extinguish.

Here are some discussion points and suggestions you can provide to parents and caregivers:

> ↵ When you come to pick up your child from school, don't ask the teacher about your child's behavior. After a long day, we all want a clean slate at home. The last thing we want to do is talk about daily problems. When the teacher is asked about behavior, it puts them in a precarious position to have to either "tattle," or frame the feedback in a way that doesn't

damage the relationship with your child. In addition, when behaviors are discussed right after school, children often get defensive.

↪ Discuss behavior and other issues at a neutral time in the evening. Once your child has had a chance to get away from school and enjoy some down time, they will be in a better frame of mind to discuss the day and be more open to your feedback and support. This is also the best time to issue consequences if they are warranted. After dinner or right before bed can be a great time to discuss concerns.

↪ Emphasize expectations of safety and learning as the reason behind behaving:

- *We pay attention so we can **learn** what the teacher is teaching.*
- *We don't hit other students because that is not **safe**. We use our words.*

↪ Avoid the trap of emphasizing punishments and/or rewards:

- *If you get a good note for paying attention, we'll go get ice cream.*
- *If you hit a student again, I'm taking away your iPad.*

↪ Consequences and occasional incentives are fine, but we don't want children behaving out of fear of punishment or the motivation to get a reward. We want them to do the right thing simply because it is the right thing to do, so focus on the behavioral expectations rather than on the resulting consequences.

↪ If the school has made you aware of an issue, don't bring it up to your child. Rather, allow them the opportunity to address the issue with you. If your child is honest and tells you what happened, praise them for being honest, while also reinforcing correct behaviors. Praising the honesty doesn't mean you are condoning the behavior, but the last thing you want is for your child to withhold information from you out of fear of punishment. Communication is critical and we want children to always feel comfortable in talking to us when concerns arise.

↪ If a behavior problem happens at school, consider having your child write an apology note. This logical consequence is appropriate, as the consequence holds the child accountable for his or her actions, while also reinforcing desired behaviors.

## If the Shoe were on the Other Foot

As a teacher working with **parents** of behaviorally at-risk students, we should approach the task with more empathy and less judgment. If you are an educator *and* parent, you understand this unique perspective, especially if you have a child with behavior concerns. By putting yourselves in the parent's place, you automatically approach the task of creating behavior change with more understanding.

Of course, it's not just the parents with whom we need to empathize. When working with **students** who are behaviorally at-risk for failure, approach the task with more empathy and less judgment, as well. Changing a behavior and breaking a habit is hard. If you have ever tried to keep a New Year's resolution you can relate. We all do the best we can, given the skills at our disposal. By putting ourselves in our students' shoes, our perspective becomes one of understanding and empathy.

## How Would You Go About Changing a Teacher's Behavior?

If you were an **administrator** in charge of changing the behavior of a teacher needing a great deal of assistance, what would you do?

### Perspective

➤ *Would you approach the task expecting it to be easy or challenging?*

➤ *Would you expect the behavior to change quickly or for the process to take time?*

➤ *Do you think the teacher would prefer encouragement or criticism?*

## Strategies

- Would you provide a list of problems you want the teacher to address or only focus on one initially?
- Would you choose a challenging goal or one that is easier to accomplish?
- Would you focus on successes or failures?

# How Would You Want Your Behavior Changed?

If the tables were turned and you were the **staff member** needing to make changes in your behavior, what type of relationship with your administrator do you think would best accomplish the goal – a healthy or strained one?

This goes back to The Behavioral Golden Rule: **Focus on changing children's behavior the way you would want your own behavior changed.** In the context of a healthy relationship, empathy and support is always more effective in creating long-term behavior change than any reward or punishment.

Dan says...

*In the context of a healthy relationship, empathy and support is always more effective in creating long-term behavior change than any reward or punishment.*

## Rewarding Poor Behavior

When it comes to changing strongly ingrained behavior habits, desperate times call for desperate measures. Mary was new to our school, and like many of my students, she had some fairly extreme behaviors. She often sat on the floor under her desk screaming at decibels I am quite sure could be heard by animals some distance away. If we tried to approach her, she usually scratched or pinched. But, if we left her alone, she went back to throwing objects until someone responded.

One day, I received a call from Mary's teacher and went to the classroom to help out. By the time I got there, the other students were being escorted out of the room for safety reasons. I worked with Mary for a while, but wasn't making much headway, when my colleague, Linda, noticed things weren't going well. She asked if she could help out. With no hesitation, my response was quick. *"Tag. You're it."* Linda was a phenomenal special education teacher who had great skills with students. *"Oh my goodness, Mr. St. Romain,"* she said in a rather loud voice. *"The fish in my fish tank are really hungry and I need someone to feed them for me. Do you know of a student who can help me?"* Of course, what was my first thought? *"No! Clearly not this child who is under her desk throwing pencils at me!"* Before I could respond, Linda leaned down. *"I'm thinking you are just the person I am looking for,"* she said to Mary. Within a few minutes, Mary calmed down and left the room with Linda, headed off to feed the fish. I'll admit I was furious at the time. *"I could have used a bribe and gotten her out from under that table, too,"* I thought.

Later that day, I spoke with Linda and explained my concern to her. *"Do we really want to reward that poor behavior by letting her feed the fish?"* I asked. She didn't hesitate with her answer. *"Is what you were doing actually working?"* She went on to explain that she believed Mary was in a state of crisis and needed a diversion in order to calm down. *"I'm using distraction, a strategy you modeled for me when I was having difficulty with one of my students."*

From that time on, when the office buzzed about Mary, Linda was called to the room for support. Sometimes she and Mary would put up a bulletin board, and at other times they would just go for a walk. It took half of the school year, but slowly the screaming went away, and the number of Mary's outbursts diminished greatly. Linda clearly changed this little girl's behavior.

When I look back, I realize Linda and I approached that situation with two completely different mindsets. While I was concerned about rewarding poor behavior, she was working to build a strong relationship of trust. This trust allowed Mary to break her poor habit of getting her needs met through screaming and throwing objects.

I think about that child and Linda often. While I was focusing on the immediate strategy, Linda was able to see the bigger picture of what was needed to help Mary find success. The story always reminds me to step back, adjust my perspective, and remember that the process of behavior change takes time.

CHAPTER TEN

# progress as a process

**Sometimes our perception becomes clouded.** It's really the only explanation I have. Teachers often come to me very frustrated. They tell me about their strategies and how unsuccessful they have been at changing behavior. Larry's third grade teacher, Miss Reynolds, was one of those individuals. She had such a difficult time with him that when the school year ended, she was so relieved Larry would be moving on to a new grade and teacher that she felt a little guilty.

But when we returned to school in August, Larry's former teacher let me know she saw him in the grocery store and was greeted with a smile from ear to ear. *"Hey, Miss Reynolds, remember me?"* he enthusiastically asked before accosting her with a massive hug. *"I was so confused,"* she said. *"That child really didn't like me."* She genuinely looked baffled. *"Knowing what I know about behavior, I'm guessing you couldn't be farther from the truth,"* I informed her. As I have to continually remind myself, it's hard to accurately assess a situation when you are in the middle of it.

## Psychological State: *A Penny for Your Thoughts?*

Are we making a difference? This is a hard question to answer because assessing behavior progress is much more challenging than evaluating academic progress. Behavior change is not as predictable or linear. In addition, behavior is just as impacted by our psychological thought process, as it is our actions. Not knowing the psychological state of the child, at times it's hard to evaluate the extent to which change is occurring or a positive difference is being made.

There are many factors impacting a child's **psychological state**:

- ↪ Relationships / Connectedness
- ↪ Trust

- Confidence Level
- Peer Relations
- Self-Esteem

We often judge the success of our interventions based only on outward behaviors. This is shortsighted. As is often the case, sometimes we are making a huge dent in the child's level of trust, but we just can't see the outward behavior change yet. We make a judgment based only on what we observe and this makes tracking improvement a difficult process.

**External Behaviors**

Unhealthy/Negative                        Healthy/Positive

**Internal Psychological State**

Untrusting/Alienated                  Trusting/Connected

For example, Larry's *external behaviors* were very unhealthy and negative, as noted above. However, by the end of the school year, I would argue he was more trusting of adults and more connected to the school staff members. In this sense, huge progress was made. But, if we only base success on outward behaviors, we miss out. This is especially the case if our goal is long-term behavioral health - as I would argue a student's internal healthy thought process is a much better indicator of progress than any external behaviors we see. As discussed earlier, observable behaviors are just the tip of the iceberg. There are many other factors to consider.

## Developmental Levels: *How old is that child, really?*

When assessing for change, we must take into consideration **developmental levels** across the spectrum impacting the behavior of our students:

- ↪ **Social Development** – A person's ability to interact with others
- ↪ **Emotional Development** – A person's ability to regulate (inhibit/exhibit) feelings
- ↪ **Ethical Development** – A person's ability to choose between right and wrong
- ↪ **Cognitive Development** – A person's intellectual functioning
- ↪ **Physical Development** – A person's age

Ever met a third grade student (emotionally and socially) trapped in the body of a fifth grader?

Maturation and regions of the brain involved in each of these areas directly affect observable behaviors. These areas also develop and mature at different times and in different ways. As is the case with cognitive development, when it comes to behavior, a student can go a long period of time somewhat "flat-lined," with regard to behavior and then one day, something clicks, and it all makes sense. *"I don't get it... I don't get it... Oh, wait. I get it!"* This can be very frustrating when trying to assess behavioral, but not noting outward progress. Children develop at their own pace and sometimes behavior change is a waiting game. Maturation will help with the process, but we have to be patient, as it takes time for this to occur.

## Control Issues: I can't do this.

As discussed earlier, we all need to feel some semblance of control in our lives. When there are factors we can't control, our behaviors often escalate. For many children, some of the behaviors they exhibit are outside their control, for a myriad of reasons. Teachers of young children observe this with students who can't seem to sit still. They can reward with stickers all day long, but if the child is unable to remain still, they will be unsuccessful at changing that behavior. We can't change what we can't control.

One good indication of a lack of control is evidenced through a child's ability to *sustain* expected behaviors. Children who have control issues will often comply with a directive immediately – but within a few minutes (or seconds), revert right back to the inappropriate behavior. Parents and teachers sometimes wrongly justify control: *"When he is doing an activity he really likes, he can pay attention fine."* Though this might be the case under highly motivating circumstances, it does not necessarily mean control is evident across the board. Many tasks we have to complete on a daily basis are not highly motivating. Unless a child exhibits control under these circumstances as well, the rationale does not hold up well.

Assessing behavioral control is not an exact science. It is a judgment call made in the context of a relationship. The more we know about a child and understand the motivation behind his or her behaviors, the better we might assess how much control is evident.

One way to examine behavior is on what I call "The Continuum of Control." On the lower end of the spectrum, the behavior is outside the realm of choice. There are multiple reasons this could be the case: reactions due to poor emotional regulation, immaturity, neurological factors or impairments, etc. Typically, the less control the child has over inappropriate behavior, the less effective traditional rewards and punishments will be. As the child gets older, negative behaviors on the lower end of this scale often become ingrained habits, which become increasingly more difficult to break.

On the other end of the continuum, the child has full control over the behavior, and simply makes poor choices. In these instances, teachers must rely on natural and logical consequences to shape behavior. When children fall into this category, it is important not to inadvertently "feed" inappropriate behaviors by dwelling on them. If the choices are being made for attention, it is easy to perpetuate the cycle by inadvertently providing more attention.

Although I do believe children of all ages make poor choices, I find the majority of students with more severe behaviors fall on the lower end of the choice spectrum. Hence, the problem with most behavior systems, which are designed with the assumption of full control and choice. Good choices are rewarded and poor choices are punished. As discussed, when a child feels as though he or she isn't in control, behaviors can be internalized (giving up, depressive affect) or externalized (lashing out, explosive affect), neither of which is a healthy response.

*I think some of my students really have impulsive behaviors they can't control, so I don't think it's fair to expect them to. I treat my students differently based on what they need and try to target goals I know they can meet. Celebrating the little successes really helps.*

– A. Duce

## Growth Mindsets – Our Beliefs, Language, and Practices

Each of the factors listed above can have a strong impact on the success of our intervention efforts. Unfortunately, we sometimes fail to look beyond the presented behaviors to the driving forces at work. I find when I take into consideration a child's internal thought process and developmental levels, as well as their ability (or lack thereof) to control behaviors, I am more understanding and patient when attempting to teach behavior skills and break habits.

Dan says...

*As we work to improve our skills in behavior management, we must assess three areas: our beliefs, our words, and our practices.*

In addition to looking at *kid* factors that impact change, we as educators also need to examine our own issues. As we work to improve our skills in behavior management, we must assess three areas: our beliefs, our words, and our practices.

# Our Beliefs

As noted in the first part of the book, our experiences shape our experiences. If our experiences of punishment effectively shaped our own behavior, we are naturally inclined to revert to punishment when faced with a student's misbehavior. Our goal should be to embrace the opportunity to teach deficit social skills and break poor habits in the context of healthy relationships.

> **Dan says...**
>
> *Our goal should be to embrace the opportunity to teach deficit social skills and break poor habits in the context of healthy relationships.*

Just as behaviors tend to fall along a continuum, so too do our beliefs. Clearly assessing the beliefs we bring into the classroom every day is the first step in changing how we approach behavioral issues. Where on each of these continuums do your beliefs about behavior management fall?

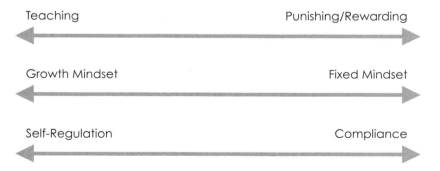

Teaching           Punishing/Rewarding

Growth Mindset           Fixed Mindset

Self-Regulation           Compliance

Beliefs can be a powerful motivator and I discovered early on in my teaching career I had several beliefs that were an Achilles Heel to my effectiveness in the classroom. They were influencing my behavior strategies, clouding my judgment and affecting my work with students:

↪ **That child doesn't care.**
I thought to myself, *"That child's not even trying. I'm bending over backwards trying to help them, and they are not doing anything."* I often made this judgment and failed to look beyond the behavior and into how the child got to this point.

↪ **That child's parent lets them get away with murder.**
*"When I was young, if I had done that in my house, my parents would have killed me."* Not having any idea of the child's home life or situation, I implicated the parents, assuming if they had just provided the right boundaries, the behavior problems would be fixed. *"If I could take that child home for a week, we wouldn't have this problem."* Of course, my perspective on this one quickly changed after the birth of our first son.

↪ **That child knows exactly what they are doing.**
I attributed the majority of behaviors to choice. *"When they want something, they can behave just fine."* I over-simplified behavior, not taking into consideration all the complex contributing factors.

↝ **We shouldn't tolerate this behavior.**
In the back of my mind, due to the way I was raised, I had a firm belief that if we just used the right punishment, we could stop the behavior. *"If the office did their job... If we would send that kid home... If we..."* I was so blinded by my beliefs; I couldn't see how my own expectation of compliance kept me from really understanding the behavior of my students.

As a teacher, the strategies I initially used were built on these beliefs. This led to frustration on my part because what I was doing wasn't working. Fortunately, throughout my educational career, I've had the opportunity to work with kids exhibiting very challenging behaviors at all levels. And these *experiences* I had completely changed my *beliefs*.

## New Beliefs About Behavior

It is only when we are willing to consider there is a better way, that we can adopt a growth-based mindset believing that behavior change for our students can be positive and ongoing:

> Dan says...
>
> *It is only when we are willing to consider there is a better way, that we can adopt a growth-based mindset...*

↝ **Behavior mainly occurs in a relationship.**
When behavior problems occur, I believe it is critical to look at all the relationships involved

and try to determine what I am doing to contribute to the situation. Rather than blaming a student, parent, or administrator, I look at all interactions and try to find ways to strengthen them.

**Implication:** *Change the relationship; change the behavior.*

### ☞ Behaviors are strengthened through skill development.

Rather than looking at behaviors as the result of choice, I view them as skills to be taught and practiced. I try to find the gifts and strengths in my students, and then help them overcome their behavioral skill deficits through continual teaching and practice.

**Implication:** *Approach behavior as an opportunity to teach.*

### ☞ Behaviors are often the result of ingrained patterns.

When behaviors are repeated over and over again, habits form in the brain. A child may know what he or she is *supposed* to do, but changing strong behavioral patterns can be challenging. Rather than assuming my students always make poor *choices*, I understand some behaviors to be the result of bad *habits*. I also know the process of changing these habits takes time and continual practice.

**Implication:** *Work with students to break poor habits of behavior.*

**↰ We all do the best we can, given the skills at our disposal.**

Believing behavior to be a skill means understanding we are all at different levels of competency. When I approach behavior with this philosophy,

> Dan says...
>
> *Believing behavior to be a skill means understanding we are all at different levels of competency.*

I find myself less frustrated and more able to concentrate on positive behavioral change. **Implication:** *Assume good intent.*

As I've embraced these new beliefs, they have helped me approach behavior from a different perspective. What I was doing wasn't working. Luckily, I discovered that as my perspective and beliefs changed, so too, did my language and practices. And this is when true behavior change started to happen – for my students *and* for me.

---

Do our **beliefs** indicate a fixed mindset of punishments and rewards, or a growth mindset of realtionships and teachable moments?

# Our Words

We all fall into habits of using phrases without thinking about the specific wording. Our word choices, however, can provide a window into our belief systems. Words matter - so consider using words and phrases that align with a positive behavioral philosophy:

Use **Inclusive Language**, which sends a collaborative message, rather than words that might be interpreted as punitive or accusatory. We want our language to shape the idea of "working with" rather than "doing to."

| Say: | Rather than Saying: |
|---|---|
| Let's clean up our area before we go to lunch. | I need you to clean up your area. |
| How can we fix this problem? | How are you going to fix this? |

Use language that promotes student **Ownership of Behavior.** By reframing our statements, we encourage children to see how their choices influence their consequences, both negative and positive.

| Say: | Rather than Saying: |
|---|---|
| If you use your time wisely and finish your journal, you'll probably have time to work on the iPad. | If you do your journal entry, I might let you have some time on the iPad. |
| When you raise your hand quietly you are showing me you want my attention. | I'm not going to call on you, if you keep shouting out. |

Use **Reflective Questioning** to prompt thinking about behavior-based rationales. Open-ended questions are more effective than closed statements for encouraging greater thought and reflection.

| Say: | Rather than Saying: |
| --- | --- |
| Why is it a bad idea to cut in front of him in line? | Don't cut in front of him. Move over here. |
| How do you think that makes her feel? | You hurt her feelings when you did that. |

Emphasize **Long-Range Behavior-Based Rationales,** rather than compliance-based rationales of reward/ punishment. By doing so, we help encourage intrinsic, altruistic motivation, which is our ultimate goal.

| Say: | Rather than Saying: |
| --- | --- |
| When we are loud in the halls, we disturb classes and interrupt their learning. | If you talk in the halls you're going to owe me time when we go to recess. |
| It's polite to use words like "please" and "thank you." | If you use words like please and thank you, you might get a sticker. |

Connect praise or correction to **Specific Skills.** Referencing a specific behavioral skill reinforces that specific behavior. In addition, a reference to a specific social skill is more likely to be carried over into other settings.

| Say: | Rather than Saying: |
| --- | --- |
| Nice job getting my attention quietly, Michael. | Nice job, Michael. |
| When Mrs. Beuhler calls your table, be ready to follow her directions and line up right away. | You guys need to behave in the cafeteria. |

Do the **words** we choose support a *growth mindset?*

## Our Practices

It's important to examine our practices and make certain they align with our beliefs. If our practices support a model of continual growth for skill development, we are moving in the right direction. Just as we examined our beliefs on a continuum, so too, should we examine the practices that are informed by those beliefs. Where on each of these continuums do your beliefs about behavior management fall?

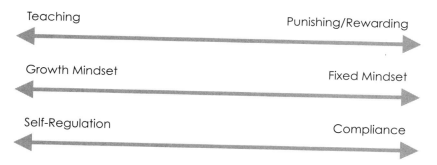

Teaching — Punishing/Rewarding

Growth Mindset — Fixed Mindset

Self-Regulation — Compliance

Do our **practices** rely on external *punishments and rewards* or natural and logical consequences rooted in healthy *relationships and teachable moments?*

# A Fresh Perspective

I was checking out at the grocery store some time ago when I looked up and recognized the cashier. It was the aunt of a student I had taught twenty years prior. I remembered her quite well, since we had to call her to pick up her niece from school on numerous occasions. Her niece would tear apart my room in no time flat when she was upset. She was one of my most challenging students and over the years I often wondered what had happened to her.

The aunt told me my former student now worked downtown at one of the big hotels and was doing great. She said she was really proud of the way her niece turned out. She also told me she couldn't say the same about any of her other nieces and nephews. We both agreed (jokingly) that her niece's success was *surely* due to the one year she had in my classroom.

I still see that aunt from time to time. She thanks me; we reminisce, laugh, and then go about our business until I see her again. Hearing about the success of my former student gives me both hope and a fresh perspective, and sometimes that's really all we need.

CHAPTER TEN

CHAPTER ELEVEN

# NOW What: Where Do I Start?

> *You have brains in your head.*
> *You have feet in your shoes.*
>
> *You can steer yourself*
> *any direction you choose!*
>
> — DR. SEUSS

**Change can be hard,** but it can also be rewarding. You don't necessarily have to burn your clip charts or throw your behavior folders into the recycling bin. The *process* of changing strategies begins by adjusting your perspective and taking small steps. Where should you start?

> **Dan says…**
>
> *The process of changing strategies begins by adjusting your perspective and taking small steps.*

1. **Target *specific* behavioral skills and teach them:**
   One of the easiest first steps is to choose a core set of skills and teach them using consistent definitions and steps. After you introduce a behavioral skill, the reinforcement of it is not something you squeeze into a single lesson. Reference it and consistently integrate it into your language each day.

2. **Have students *practice* skills as a means of breaking bad habits.**
   As with any skill, the more you practice, the better you get. If a student is in a poor pattern of behavior, the misbehavior will continue and the habit will get stronger, if the pattern is not interrupted. If our interventions focus on retraining the brain, we stand a better chance of breaking the poor habit and replacing it with the positive behavioral skill. Find specific ways to help students practice appropriate behaviors when problems arise, allowing natural and logical consequences to help shape behaviors.

3. **Assess and discuss progress *continually*.**
   Work with students and have ongoing discussions about progress. This is a critical step in the process of change. The more we make children aware of their behavior patterns, the better chance they have of changing them. Targeted discussions provide opportunities for goal setting, reflection, and continued teachable moments. Positive discussions also serve to strengthen your relationships, increasing the likelihood change will occur.

**4. Focus on *acknowledging* good choices, rather than rewarding them.**

If our goal is to help students focus on making good choices, it is important we don't inadvertently shift this focus by continuously offering rewards for positive behaviors. When possible, use intermittent acknowledgements and ongoing encouragement to strengthen positive behaviors.

**5. Work *together* as a team.**

The beauty of teaching in a school setting is that you have a built-in support system of colleagues around you. Consider meeting with your grade level team to brainstorm strategies to use with different students. For example, you could have a student work in another classroom with a different teacher for a short time, giving you both a break.

**6. Be *patient*. Changing behavior takes time.**

Our Special Education Director once told me, *"Dan, if you try to judge your effectiveness based on how these kids behave, you are in for a long, painful, and sad career in education."* She laughed and told me I needed to adjust my perspective. *"You are just adding another layer of support in the long line of teachers trying to help these kids do well when they become adults."* She had a good point. At the time, I remember being so focused on wanting to see immediate change in their behavior while they were with me, that I failed to remember my ultimate goal - for them to succeed once they leave the school system altogether.

*It has been my experience as an administrator, who has worked closely with Dan for the past twenty years, that with small shifts in perspectives and strategies, grounded in a culture of continuous improvement, we can change behavior and make our schools a better place for our children.*

– S. Peery

# You Can Do This

*"You sold me. I was on the brink of retirement and worn out trying to deal with all the problems in my class, until I started focusing on teaching behavior skills and breaking habits. Now, I like my job again, and as a result, I'm not planning on retiring anytime soon."* It was probably the best validation of my work I could have received. Last year, a teacher approached me and these were the first words out of her mouth. She had heard me speak on several occasions and as a result, changed her approach in dealing with student behaviors. *"Your strategies were good, but what I needed was the perspective shift. It was a game changer. I hadn't realized how much my own perspective was working against me. And by the way, I was one of 'those' teachers. So, if I can do it, anybody can."* Before I could ask her to elaborate, she turned and walked off with a spring in her step, and I walked away motivated to get this book written.

Over the years, I have heard many variations of this type of positive feedback from teachers. Of course, this encourages me to know that behavior change is not only possible; it is happening. I often tell people, "I **like** working with kids, but **love** working with adults." For just as teachers enjoy watching students have "aha" moments when the light bulbs click – I get energized when teachers have their own "aha" moments. Why? Because as an educator, and the father of a son with behavior concerns, I've had my own "aha" moments.

> Dan says...
>
> *...behavior change is not only possible; it is happening.*

Based on personal experience, as well as the feedback I have received from others, I am convinced you too can achieve a transformation that will better prepare your students to succeed, not just in your classroom, but in life. When you commit yourself to letting go of systems that haven't worked for your students... when you open yourself to a positive mindset... when you embrace growth... you *can* build better behavior in your classroom. And you can do it a way that plays to your strength... teaching.

The process of changing our approach can be challenging, but when the changes result in better behavioral skills and self-empowerment for your students, I truly believe the results are worth the effort.

# Resources

I feel fortunate to have been exposed to a great deal of excellent professional development in my career. Listed below are individuals and organizations that have shaped my thinking and skill set. All resources in this list support the idea of strengthening student behavior through by teaching skills in the context of healthy relationships.

**BOOKS:**

***Beyond Discipline: From Compliance to Community*** by Alfie Kohn

This book is an easy read, but very thought provoking. Alfie Kohn has several other books that challenge widely accepted claims, but this is my favorite.

***Brain-Based Learning*** by Eric Jensen

Eric is an amazing man with a great passion for teaching and learning. I quote him often as saying, *"The best kind of discipline is the kind nobody notices."* He has numerous books out for educators.

***Conscious Discipline*** by Becky Bailey

I'm a big fan of Becky Baily's work. She offers great information and practical advice for meeting the social-emotional needs of children in schools.

***Daring Greatly: How the Courage to Be Vulnerable Transforms the Way We Live, Love, Parent, and Lead*** by Brene Brown

Brene Brown has written several bes-sellers. Her work on empathy is powerful.

***Drive: The Surprising Truth about What Motivates Us*** by Daniel Pink

***Drive*** offers a great deal of research on motivation, and specifically, how external rewards can work against our efforts. I believe there is much to be learned by examining the implications of his information for the school setting.

**_Just Because it's Not Wrong Doesn't Make it Right:_ _Teaching Kids to Think and Act Ethically_** by Barbara Coloroso

I heard Barbara Coloroso speak on this topic when this book came out. She has great insight into encouraging ethical behavior in our kids.

**_Visible Learning_** by John Hattie

John Hattie synthesizes tons of data and provides recommendations on best practices for educators. He emphasizes the importance of the teacher-student relationship in the learning process.


## ORGANIZATIONS:

### The Boys Town Model of Social Skills

This organization has great resources and workshops for supporting challenging behaviors in the school setting. There is also an excellent parent training component to the model, _Common Sense Parenting._

### Character Education Partnership (character.org)

This organization provides countless information on ways to support character education and behavior. Specifically, the organization developed _11 Principles of Character Education,_ which is a great resource for strengthening efforts regarding school discipline.

### Positive Behavioral Interventions and Supports (PBIS)

This body of work provides evidence-based recommendations for behavioral best practices in schools. I've worked with many schools on implementing this initiative. It is an excellent resource for designing expectations in classroom and school settings.

# Acknowledgements

I discovered the process of writing this book was very stressful. I finished it at midnight on Easter morning, but did the majority of my writing the forty days leading up to that point. How fitting that at times I felt as though I was wandering in the desert. Lucky for me, I had a huge support system of individuals who carried me through the process.

First, I must thank my family. My wife, Prissy, models what I teach without even trying. Her love and unspoken contributions inspired me when it all started to become a blur. And my boys, Matthieu, Micah, Marc and Max, each with their own unique gifts and challenges, who broadened my understanding of behavior - and continue to do so.

Thanks also to several of my friends and family who endured many a discussion about behavior. Lee Anne and Cecile were my two biggest cheerleaders, and they kept my business afloat while I was knee-deep in writing mode. Cheryl spent countless hours on the phone with me pouring through the final draft before it was turned in. And just knowing I could call Laura, Todd, Libby, and my siblings at any time meant a great deal to me.

As mentioned in the dedication, I'm appreciative of my Howard family, and specifically, Wilma, Dan, Stephanie, and Susan, the principals who challenged me professionally. I am also thankful for the input provided by Peggy, Marianne, and Mary Ellen. I bent their ears many times throughout the writing process.

Lastly, a huge thank you goes out to my NCYI extended family - Jennifer, Robert, Jason, Phillip, and my editor, Matt. Without their ongoing encouragement and support, this book would not have been written. They kept me on schedule and dealt with my many obsessive issues too numerous to list.

I am blessed beyond measure and thankful for you all.

# About the Author

Dan St. Romain is a national independent educational consultant who provides staff development and consultative services to educators working with students at all levels. Dan is passionate about helping educators shift their perspective on discipline, understanding the best ways to provide support given the challenges posed in today's society.

After receiving his Master's degree in Education, Dan worked in both private residential and public school settings. His work as a self-contained behavior unit teacher, Educational Diagnostician, and Director of a Learning Resource Center has afforded him experience at all levels, in both general and special education settings.

Currently, Dan is a behavior consultant for the Alamo Heights Independent School District in San Antonio, Texas, working directly with students, while also providing support to the staff, at large. Though Dan travels a great deal presenting nationally throughout the school year and during the summer, he looks forward to spending holiday time with family and their yearly beach vacation with close friends.

**Connect with Dan at:**

www.danstromain.com

dan@danstromain.com

Twitter @danstromain

# Social Skills Resources
# from Dan St. Romain

Available at **ncyi.org**
and **danstromain.com**.